'This book provides a clearly written
personal qualities needed to try to save lives at risk from suicide. _
it's not on your course reading list it should be: I haven't seen a better
description of how always to have hope, maintain that when others have
none, and to value all human life as if it were a member of your family.'

     – Vivien Isaac-Curson, a retired Psychiatric
Nurse and Clinical Co-Ordinator

'This invaluable book is not a top-down medicalised view of how to save
lives but rather a compassionate account of immensely practical lessons
from someone who has experienced suicidal crisis and has used her
knowledge and understanding to so effectively support others.'

     – Dr Heather Castillo, author of Personality Disorder Temperament
or Trauma? *and* The Reality of Recovery in Personality Disorder

'This is a much needed and welcome publication. Joy sets out in such a
clear and compelling way just why and how we can better care for some
of the most vulnerable members of our society. Joy, very movingly at
times, draws on her personal experience and the invaluable work she
and her team have done over the years and sets out steps to help those
at risk of suicide. This book should be compulsory reading for all those
who work with and care for those vulnerable to suicide. We can and
must do more.'

     – Steven Powles is a barrister at Doughty Street Chambers. He
has worked with Joy in helping families who have lost someone
to suicide navigate their way through the inquest process.

SUICIDE PREVENTION TECHNIQUES

of related interest

New Approaches to Preventing Suicide
A Manual for Practitioners
Edited by David Duffy and Tony Ryan
ISBN 978 1 84310 221 2
eISBN 978 1 84642 010 8

A Comprehensive Guide to Suicidal Behaviours
Working with Individuals at Risk and their Families
David Aldridge and Sergio Pérez Barrero
ISBN 978 1 84905 025 8
eISBN 978 0 85700 515 1

Working with Suicidal Individuals
A Guide to Providing Understanding, Assessment and Support
Tony White
ISBN 978 1 84905 115 6
eISBN 978 0 85700 224 2

After the Suicide
Helping the Bereaved to Find a Path from Grief to Recovery
Kari Dyregrov, Einar Plyhn and Gudrun Dieserud
ISBN 978 1 84905 211 5
eISBN 978 0 85700 445 1

Things Jon Didn't Know About
Our Life After My Husband's Suicide
Sue Henderson
ISBN 978 1 78592 400 2
eISBN 978 1 78450 766 4

I'll Write Your Name on Every Beach
A Mother's Quest for Comfort, Courage and Clarity After Suicide Loss
Susan Auerbach
ISBN 978 1 78592 758 4
eISBN 978 1 78450 615 5

SUICIDE
PREVENTION
TECHNIQUES

HOW A
SUICIDE CRISIS SERVICE
SAVES LIVES

JOY HIBBINS

Jessica Kingsley *Publishers*
London and Philadelphia

The author's royalties for this book are being donated to the charity Suicide Crisis.

First published in 2019
by Jessica Kingsley Publishers
73 Collier Street
London N1 9BE, UK
and
400 Market Street, Suite 400
Philadelphia, PA 19106, USA

www.jkp.com

Library of Congress Cataloging in Publication Data
A CIP catalog record for this book is available from the Library of Congress

British Library Cataloguing in Publication Data
A CIP catalogue record for this book is available from the British Library

ISBN 978 1 78592 549 8
eISBN 978 1 78450 949 1

Printed and bound in Great Britain

CONTENTS

Please note that the names of clients have been changed throughout the book.

INTRODUCTION TO THE AUTHOR

Joy's tireless dedication to providing safe, supportive and therapeutic help for people thinking about suicide has led to the Suicide Crisis Centre and numerous presentations, blogs and newsletters that reach and inform people from all sectors. Her thoughtful assimilation of personal experience, experience of those who use her service, evidence and policy, and opinions of others in the field is informative and stimulating. Joy's work is rooted in her values of collaboration and she has developed strong and productive relationships with the clients she serves and with healthcare providers and other agencies involved in the suicide prevention endeavour. It has been a privilege to get to know and to learn from Joy and I look forward to adding to my knowledge and understanding by reading her book.

Karen Lascelles
Nurse Consultant Suicide Prevention,
Oxford Health NHS Foundation Trust

CHAPTER I

LIVED EXPERIENCE

HOW IT IMPACTS ON OUR SERVICES

If I had not experienced suicidal crisis myself, I would not have gained the knowledge and understanding which allowed me to set up a service which was not only innovative, but which truly met the needs of our clients.

In March 2012, a deeply traumatic experience changed my life. During the experience I felt shock, horror and fear. Within hours of the event, I started to experience flashbacks and intrusive thoughts: symptoms of post-traumatic stress disorder (PTSD). The symptoms became overwhelming. Memories of the event returned uninvited. I could neither process what had happened to me, nor escape from the memories of it. As the days passed, I started to have suicidal thoughts. This was the beginning of a suicidal crisis that led to community mental health crisis support, and, ultimately, psychiatric hospital admission.

I had not experienced psychiatric services prior to 2012. Initially, an on-call doctor referred me to the crisis team, otherwise known as the crisis resolution and home treatment team.

The crisis team is a community psychiatric team which provides home visits to people under their care. They usually visit every day when the person is in crisis. The service was set up as an alternative to psychiatric hospital.

I struggled to engage with the team. A different crisis team member would come out to see me every day. The usual practice was for eight or more team members to be involved. They would visit on rotation. With a huge caseload and limited time, they rarely had the opportunity to read up more than the previous day's notes about me. This meant that some of them did not know what had triggered my crisis. As a result, I had to repeat traumatic information again and again to different team members, which meant that I was reliving the event multiple times and re-experiencing the horror of it.

When you have experienced something traumatic, your ability to trust people may evaporate. In the period after such a trauma, it can be difficult enough to build up trust with one person, let alone a whole team. This made connecting with the crisis team challenging for me. The team recognised this and tried to limit the number who visited me, but shifts and staff shortages made that impossible.

Additionally, when multiple team members are involved, it can lead to a lack of continuity of care.

The clinical distance of psychiatric staff proved challenging for me. I understand why such distance exists, and I will explore that later in the book. However, it left me equally detached and disengaged.

On one occasion, a crisis team member arrived at my home, came into the dining room and took one of the chairs away from the table in order to sit at the far end of the room, at the furthest possible distance from me. It was an act which served as a powerful symbol of the gulf between us.

One of the effects of a traumatic event is that it can subsequently lead to a need to feel in control. During the traumatic experience, you may have been rendered powerless, and may have felt a total loss of control over what was happening. That is a feeling that you may never wish to replicate. However, as a patient under psychiatric services you can often feel that the power is removed from you, and that it lies with the psychiatric service and its clinicians. There is a significant power imbalance between psychiatrist and patient. Additionally, the community psychiatric teams (such as the crisis team) decided how often the team would see me and the kind of treatments and care I would receive. They also decided when to discharge me. Significantly, I still felt at risk of suicide at the point when I was discharged.

At the same time (apart from when I was detained under the Mental Health Act (passed in 1983) or 'sectioned'), I was told directly that it was 'my choice' or 'my decision' to end my life. This was a profoundly unhelpful message, which I felt validated the decision to die. It was clearly not the intention of the clinicians that their words should be interpreted in this way.

It seemed as though I had total freedom of choice over whether to live or die – but no choice about the kind of psychiatric care I received, or the services I could access. These were just some of the aspects of psychiatric care which made engagement difficult for me. It became clear to me that there was a need for a different kind of crisis care – one which would involve using different techniques and strategies from those of the crisis team. We would also interact and communicate with clients in an entirely different way. Furthermore, we would alter the power balance between professional and client, empowering and giving autonomy to the client but actively intervening to keep them safe when they were in crisis, whether or not they had the mental capacity to make decisions. Our focus would be on working tenaciously to help them stay alive throughout the time that they were under our services.

Instead of maintaining clinical distance, we would openly care for our clients, recognising the power of kindness and care in reaching a person at the point of suicide. We would demonstrate that caring for clients is not incompatible with a professional relationship which has clear boundaries. We would find ways to reach people who were off the radar of other services; people who other services were describing as 'hard to reach'. We would engage people who were described as 'difficult to engage'.

Having identified that there were sometimes gaps in the current mental health system through which people could fall, we would seek to eradicate them, creating a safety net around our clients which would keep them safe. Importantly, we would respond to a crisis wherever it occurred. Throughout all this, the lived experience perspective would remain at the heart of our work.

Ultimately, it was not just my own experience of suicidal crisis which influenced the way we work at the Suicide Crisis Centre. It was also the experiences of our first few clients, who helped shape the services we now provide. In assessing their individual needs, it became clear that we would have to adapt our services, and provide additional ones, to ensure that we met their needs – and to ensure that they survived.

My lived experience has an enduring impact on my work. Although formal training has been vital, my own experience has given me a depth and breadth of knowledge which I draw upon regularly. It also gives me a profound empathy with our clients' experiences, and a deep understanding of what it is like to be in crisis.

CHAPTER 2

THE RELATIONSHIP WITH CLIENTS

BUILDING A STRONG CONNECTION WITH CLIENTS

The clinical distance I experienced under mental health services left me detached, disengaged – and at greater risk, as a result.

It is not unusual for a person to disconnect from the people around them in the lead-up to a suicide attempt. During a depressive illness, they may withdraw from the world and isolate themselves. If they start to develop suicidal thoughts, they may detach further. As the emotional pain and feelings of hopelessness increase, they may experience a form of tunnel vision which renders them temporarily unable to hold their loved ones in their mind. At this point, professionals may need to work tenaciously to help them to stay connected to life.

A caring approach can have an extraordinary effect at such times. Kindness has the power to break through the barriers you may have carefully constructed around yourself, as you seek to detach from life. I learned this myself while on a general hospital ward in 2012. I was admitted to the ward overnight, because staff were concerned about my suicide risk. The staff on the ward were kind, concerned and attentive, and I received the strong impression that my survival mattered to them. Moreover, their caring approach reconnected me with an aspect of life that I had lost sight of in the darkness of my depression. They reminded me of the good that exists in people

– the kindness, compassion and wish to help which represent the best of human nature. That helped me to reconnect with life. I started to feel that this was perhaps a world in which I wanted to remain.

At the Crisis Centre, the way we work with our clients is very similar: we care about them. We rarely need to *say* that we care and, indeed, it is often they who tell us that they know we do. Our care is evident from the way in which we interact with them, the time and attention we give them and the things we do to try to ensure their survival.

We do what we can to help with aspects of their life which are causing them pain. We do this instinctively. But of course, these are often the aspects of their life which are impacting on their suicide risk.

Amelia came to us after losing custody of her children to her ex-husband. The loss of her children was devastating, particularly as her mental health had been cited in court as one of the reasons why she should not care for them anymore. She had to attend a number of court hearings to gain further access to her children, and her distress intensified in the weeks leading up to them, not least because she would have to face her ex-partner in court. It was important that as well as providing regular appointments for her at our Suicide Crisis Centre, we also attended family court hearings and supported her through the process.

One of the required actions to have greater access to her children was to undertake a parenting course. However, Amelia had not been able to meet this requirement. She explained to us that she needed literacy support to complete the course but did not know how to access it. She was deeply depressed, and it felt like an overwhelming hurdle to overcome. Fortunately, one of our team had worked as an adult literacy teacher in the past. School had been a difficult experience for Amelia, but the one-to-one literacy support, from a person she trusted, enabled her to work through the course and complete it.

The loss of her children had profoundly damaged Amelia's sense of self-worth. During the court process her parenting abilities had been called into question. It had, however, been abundantly clear to me from our first meeting that she was a loving, caring parent who always put the interests of her children first. She had older children who remained in her care, all of them compassionate, responsible young people who were doing well at college and at work. They were respected and valued by their course tutors and employers. This was powerful evidence of her parenting skills. We helped her to identify the evidence that she could present to the court and social services to reassure them of her ability to care for her children. We also helped her to recognise the personal qualities she possessed that made her a good parent. Ultimately, she gained far greater access to her children.

Amelia had found it difficult to access mental health services. Her main contact apart from us was with her family doctor. However, a significant percentage of our clients have previously been under mental health services, most usually under the crisis team. Some have commented that they didn't have a sense of being cared for under that team. It was not just the clinical distance which gave this impression. They also cited other factors that had led them to form this view. They told us that when another service (such as the police, ambulance crew or charitable organisation) contacted the crisis team to express concerns about their suicide risk, the response of the team was usually, 'The patient is welcome to call us' or 'They know our number and can call us any time.' The aim of this is perhaps to give the person greater autonomy, or to encourage them to take an active role in trying to manage their own crisis. However, it gave the impression that the crisis team was not concerned about them. They could not understand why the team did not seek to contact them after concerns had been raised by another service about their suicide risk.

Sometimes I am invited by the local mental health service to attend meetings of professionals relating to the care of a patient, if we are also supporting them. In one such meeting, I recall the patient commenting that she felt that no one within her mental health team cared whether she lived or died. The clinicians present at the meeting did not respond to her comment. It was evident from communications I had with one of the clinicians afterwards that they did indeed care very much. They were explicit about this. I found the communication from the clinician extremely poignant and moving. I also felt huge sadness. There appeared to be a gulf between them: the clinicians cared, but the patient did not know this at all.

I can understand that there are many reasons why mental health clinicians may seek to maintain a clinical distance from their patients. It may be partly for self-protection; to prevent the clinician from becoming too involved and to protect against the emotional distress of losing a patient. However, there also seems to be a fear among many clinicians of openly caring about patients. Indeed, a mental health clinician voiced this to me in the summer of 2012, on a night when I was considered to be at imminent risk.

I had phoned the crisis team and they were concerned about my level of distress and my proximity to a suicide method which I was intending to use that night. The crisis team nurse at the end of the phone was concerned that I was going to end my life and she said, 'I'm not afraid to say that I care.' It is interesting that she made reference to fear. The implication was that her colleagues *were* afraid to openly acknowledge that they cared. This fear may originate in part from a concern that caring could be misinterpreted by patients, and that it could blur the boundaries of the relationship between the clinician and the patient.

In our experience, that is not what happens. Clients understand that it is a professional relationship. It is absolutely possible to combine professionalism with caring. The two are not incompatible.

There are many aspects of the client experience which can help to establish clear boundaries. Within our service, appointments are time-limited and generally last for an hour, unless someone is at imminent risk.

As well as creating boundaries of time, we also ensure that the boundaries between our personal and professional lives are clearly defined. Clients do not have access to the personal phone numbers of our team members, and indeed our team members do not have individual work phone numbers. All phone contact from clients comes through a central system.

It would also be extremely rare for us to share personal experience in appointments with clients. The focus is on them and on their experience.

There are times when limited sharing can be helpful. One night I went out to see Ed, a client we had been supporting for a few weeks, because we were concerned about him being at risk of suicide. His distress had increased markedly because there was a tribunal scheduled for the following day that would determine whether his welfare benefits could be reinstated. He was having strong thoughts of ending his life that night because he felt that he could not face the ordeal of the tribunal. He was convinced that the tribunal panel would uphold the decision to terminate his benefits. The potential loss of benefits was not what had caused his suicidal crisis originally, but it had caused an escalation of his risk at this particular time.

Ed spoke that night about the original trigger for his crisis: a traumatic event which had led to the emergence of PTSD. He was under secondary mental health services but had been waiting to access psychological therapy. He felt overwhelmed by his symptoms at times. As we were talking, Ed became increasingly angry. At one point, he said, 'None of you professionals really understands what it is like to have PTSD.' I considered Ed to be at high risk that night, and I felt that he was starting to feel a gulf between him and the 'professionals'. I told him that I did understand, because I had been diagnosed with PTSD in the past. He asked me one question in relation to this – a general question rather than a personal one – which I answered. He was extremely surprised to hear that someone who was there to help him had also experienced this disorder. He subsequently told me that it had really helped him. The fact that I was working full time and functioning well gave him hope. He had assumed that it would not be possible to recover. Now he felt that he might.

The knowledge that the person supporting them has lived experience can be helpful, but the detailed sharing of the helper's lived experience would risk changing the relationship.

I recall that in the early days of providing our services, a professional referring a client to us misunderstood the role and purpose of our organisation. She had read in a newspaper that our Suicide Crisis Centre had been set up by a person with lived experience, and she informed the client that we were an organisation staffed by people who had been through suicidal crisis, whose role was to demonstrate to clients, by our example, that it was possible to survive it. This was a misapprehension, because our team is not made up specifically of people who have experienced crisis themselves. Additionally, the service she described would make the staff member's experience of crisis a focal point – the opposite of what we do. Furthermore, the knowledge that another person has been able to survive a crisis does not necessarily comfort, encourage or reassure someone who is currently in crisis.

There are services in which lived experience is central to the supporting role. Peer support services are becoming increasingly prevalent and are proving to be hugely beneficial, but this is different from what we are providing.

Maintaining clear boundaries ensures that clients do not interpret our caring for them to indicate that we are providing friendship. Interestingly, though, some highly successful third-sector organisations, including some services specifically working with people in suicidal crisis, describe the type of support which they provide as 'befriending'. Such services are often more short term than ours, and that may be why they feel able to use the term – they may support for a few days but have no further contact. However, this is not a term we use. Firstly, we feel that there would be a risk of our clients misunderstanding this and assuming that we were offering friendship, which is a more personal relationship. Secondly, 'befriending' would not seem to accurately describe the work that our team members are undertaking and the fact that they have received several years of training. We are using professional techniques to help our clients during appointments. That is why many of our clients refer to us as counsellors, even though we generally use the term Suicide Crisis team member.

CREATING AN ENDURING CONNECTION

In building a strong connection with our clients, it is important that only a very small team works with them. I had experienced the involvement of multiple staff members when I was under the crisis team and recognised how it had affected my ability to engage with them. As a result, we usually ensure that only two members of our team work with each client. This allows us to build trust, create a strong connection, get to know the client well and provide continuity of care.

We see most of our clients for an hour a day on consecutive days during the acute phase of their crisis. This is similar to the amount of time the mental health crisis team allocates to its patients. However, we know that patients are not always surviving under the crisis teams. The University of Manchester's *National Confidential Inquiry into Suicide and Homicide by People with Mental Illness* (Appleby *et al.* 2016) confirmed that around three times as many people die under the care of crisis teams as in psychiatric hospitals.

In my opinion, one of the reasons why our clients survive is because of the strong relationship and connection we build with them. If the quality of the relationship is good, it can sustain a person even when the professional is absent. A client wrote a particularly memorable quote on the Suicide Crisis Facebook page which emphasises this: 'You remain in my pocket for life, supporting, guiding and aiding my recovery.' The image 'in my pocket' highlights the fact that he feels we are always with him. He feels supported, even when he is not with us. Significantly, he describes this as being 'for life'. The connection is strong enough to continue after a person has left our services. He indicates that it continues to have an impact.

For 23 hours of the day, the client may not be with us. But during that time, they still feel that they are cared for, supported and that if things deteriorate, they can immediately contact the service, and we will respond.

This strong relationship is the reason why they will phone our emergency line when they are at the point of suicide, even if they would not have sought help from another service at that moment. John called our emergency line in the early hours of the morning. He was on his way to the location where he intended to end his life. I recall that it was a winter's night with strong winds and driving rain. We talked for a considerable amount of time, and I remained on the phone to him as he walked back to the main road and made the long journey home. Afterwards, he explained that he would not have called another service at that point. 'I could not have ended my life without talking to you first. You have done so much for me.'

His comment 'you have done so much for me' seems to relate to the actions which we instinctively take, partly to help the person to survive, but also because we care enough to do them. He may have been referring to the amount of time and attention we had devoted to his care.

The breakup of his marriage had triggered his suicidal crisis initially. One of the aspects of single life that was particularly difficult for him was returning to an empty house after work. He felt profoundly alone at such times.

It became clear that he found it helpful to express his deep emotional pain in writing, and he started to send a daily email to our charity. We ensured that there was a reply from us waiting when he arrived home from work every evening. He said this helped, because he would be anticipating our email waiting for him, rather than focusing on the emptiness of the home. In a symbolic sense, someone would be 'there' for him on his return home. This daily email contact also built a strong connection with us. He was able to share his innermost feelings and fears with a team he trusted.

It is important that clients feel a connection with us even after they have left our service, because they may need to return one day. We cannot assume that a person will only experience a suicidal crisis once in their life.

John appeared to recover well from his original crisis. He moved to a different area, made new friends and started a new job which brought him into contact with people regularly. His previous job had involved working alone and had contributed to his feeling of isolation after the relationship breakup. One evening, however, more than a year after his original contact with us, we received a text message which said simply, 'Can I come to see you now?' We arranged to see him immediately, and initially he found it difficult to communicate at all. We spent an extensive amount of time with him that night, and he was able to explain that his cousin had died. He had been extremely close to her, and indeed she had been a huge source of support to him during his suicidal crisis the previous year. Initially, he had acted in the way he always did after the death of a family member: he looked after everyone else. He dedicated most of his days to providing emotional support to her family, who were equally bereft. During this period, his own grief was suppressed. As the weeks went on, his own feelings of loss started to emerge. He had always described the loss of his partner as akin to a bereavement, and now he was grieving for the two people to whom he had been closest. John told us that his team at Suicide Crisis were now the people he trusted most in life. As well as providing a constant, reliable and stable presence in his life, we also fulfilled a vital role in terms of being able to openly care about him at a time when his sense of isolation was acute.

Sometimes there are particular reasons why we may need to work to maintain the connection after clients leave our services. They may need to access long-term specialist treatment in other settings, such as inpatient units designed for people who have a particular diagnosis, or addiction rehabilitation services. They may be vulnerable on discharge, when they return home after receiving such intensive support in a residential setting. It is important that they know we will be there at that time. Keeping in contact with them during their stay maintains the connection and helps reassure them that they will be supported when they return to living in the community. This contact is equally important if a client receives a prison sentence.

Calum, one of our clients, has been in prison for the past year and I have kept in regular contact with both him and his mother throughout this time. I was beside his mother in the public gallery of the court on the day he was convicted and I shared her shock at the sentence he received. We had both been expecting that he would receive a drug rehabilitation order instead, because the judge at his previous court hearing had requested that this be explored. The judge had said it would be important to locate a rehabilitation centre where he could receive treatment not just for addiction but also for his mental health issues. A rehabilitation centre had agreed to offer such a six-month admission for him, and they were ready to receive him as a patient. However, the judge at the final hearing took a very different view and decided to impose a prison sentence instead. We were extremely concerned about him being at risk of suicide during those first few days in custody and we made regular calls to prison staff.

Initially devastated, Calum took time to quietly process and reflect on his sentence, and it was not long before he told us that he felt it was right that he served a sentence. He had heard the impact statements of victims which were read out in court and felt deeply shocked at the effect on them and extremely remorseful for what he had done.

Life in prison has been extremely hard for him at times. He made exceptional progress for many months, volunteering for a listening service which provides support to other prisoners. However, his mental health deteriorated when his medication was changed. At this point, he started to self-harm and withdrew from his loved ones, refusing all contact for some time. Such times of silence are deeply worrying for families. I understand now the feeling of powerlessness that they experience. We cannot immediately go and see him, or phone or text. We can only voice our concerns to prison staff and wait for news.

Even during Calum's periods of silence, we have continued to write. It is important that he knows we remain here for him.

Connection with clients is built through communication in all its forms, and listening is an extremely important part of this. Only by really listening and understanding can we start to know how to help. A journalist recently asked me to give examples of phrases we use when talking to a person who is at risk of suicide, believing that this would be helpful to pass on to readers. We do use some phrases which are known to be effective in establishing and assessing the person's suicide risk. However, we do not use set phrases when it comes to supporting and helping our clients, because we are responding to individuals. They are unique and their crisis – both in its manifestation and circumstances – is unique to them. What we say to a client will depend on what we have heard them say, and on what we have learned about them and their situation.

RECOGNISING THE EXPERIENCE OF THE INDIVIDUAL

I learned how important it is to listen attentively and really hear the client from my own experiences of being under services.

When I was detained under Section 2 of the Mental Health Act (1983) in a psychiatric hospital ('sectioned'), I felt trapped and imprisoned. I could not escape. This replicated aspects of the traumatic experience that had triggered my mental health crisis originally. It was as if I was reliving the experience on a daily basis, and this created a kind of inner torment that felt unbearable. I expressed this to a member of the nursing staff at the psychiatric hospital and her response was: 'I know this is frustrating for you.' Despite my clear expression of inner torment, the nurse had apparently not heard this. She appeared to have made an assumption that the response people feel, when sectioned, is frustration. Perhaps she had witnessed patients expressing frustration at the restrictions that sectioning placed on them. Perhaps she imagined that she would find being sectioned frustrating. Whatever the reason, her preconceptions meant that she was unable to hear my individual response to sectioning. As a result, she was unable to provide appropriate help. Importantly, it meant that she did not realise that my mental anguish had caused my risk of suicide to escalate while I was in the psychiatric hospital.

My own personal experiences showed me how important it was to really focus on our clients' individual experiences. I realised that counselling training was central to this. One of the core skills we learn in the early stages of training is how to reflect back to the client the emotions and feelings that we hear them expressing. This ensures that the person feels really heard, and that we have understood the impact of significant events on them, and the extent and depth of their emotional response. Although we are providing crisis support, not counselling, the skills learned in counselling training are highly relevant to our work.

Clients generally respond extremely powerfully to hearing their emotions reflected back to them. They are immediately aware that we fully understand and empathise with what they are feeling.

Paraphrasing and summarising are other skills learned in counselling training, and these allow us to feed back to the client our understanding of the circumstances and events which they have described to us. The client can then confirm our understanding or correct it. This is extremely important. I requested copies of my psychiatric records this year and was surprised by the number of factual errors, including clear evidence of some staff members' inaccurate understanding of the events and circumstances which led to my suicidal crisis.

In 2016, I was invited to give oral evidence to the Parliamentary Health Select Committee which was undertaking an inquiry into the measures needed to prevent suicide (Health Select Committee 8 November 2016). I was subsequently asked by the Committee to provide further evidence by commenting on the government's suicide prevention strategy. One of the suggestions I made was that crisis team staff should have training in these basic counselling skills. Some of the basic skills could be taught in a matter of hours.

Increasingly, psychiatrists are recognising the importance of these skills. If we can arrange for psychiatric nursing staff to be equipped with them too, it could help to ensure that the individual experiences of patients are understood and validated.

PROVIDING INDIVIDUALISED CARE

Our clients sometimes describe feeling that they have encountered a generalised approach from staff within the crisis team, when they have contacted them, rather than a response specifically tailored to their individual situation. I recognise the highly skilled and effective work undertaken by our mental health crisis teams, but wonder whether the remit given to them is perhaps too restrictive, preventing them from using different techniques to help patients.

There is a particular emphasis placed on 'distraction techniques'. These are activities which are intended to divert your mind away from distressing thoughts, and they can be extremely beneficial. However, if it is assumed that they are appropriate for everyone, in every situation, they may be less helpful. I learned this from my own experience of crisis in 2012. I phoned the crisis team and was asked immediately, 'What are you going to do to distract yourself?' There followed some suggestions of activities I might undertake, but I had wanted my individual experience to be acknowledged and understood at that point, rather than being given such general advice.

Joanna, one of our clients, described phoning the crisis team after receiving extremely upsetting news about her physical health, which would have lasting implications for her:

> I remember calling the crisis team once when I had just come out of hospital. I was terribly upset about the news I'd just been given and, in combination with my mental health issues and other life events, I was feeling actively suicidal. The person who took the call stuck very firmly to what I call 'the script' and made suggestions to me such as to go home and make a cup of tea. I was crying to them down the phone and repeated how I wanted to end my life there and then. At that point, I ended the conversation and broke down in the hospital car park where a parked ambulance paramedic saw my distress and convinced me to walk into the emergency department and tell them I was feeling suicidal.

It is important to be able to recognise that a person may reach a point when they can no longer rely on distraction techniques and that a different type of response or intervention is needed.

There are of course many examples of crisis team members adopting a much more individualised approach, and indeed I encountered such a team member in 2012. His focus was on allowing me to ventilate my emotions, and although this was painful, it was ultimately helpful. He showed significant empathy. Ten days before I experienced the life-changing and destabilising traumatic event which had triggered my crisis, I had lost my mother. He told me that he had lost his father and understood the impact of the death of a parent. His self-disclosure was limited, but effective in establishing a connection. On his first visit, he explained that I would be seen daily by a member of his team, 'Every day someone will come out to see you who cares about you.' This was an extraordinarily powerful phrase, and it was one of only two occasions where I heard a mental health clinician feel able to use the word 'care' in relation to a patient. I learned from this experience what a powerful impact it can have when you know that professionals care about you.

Clients have described feeling that a generalised approach may also be adopted in the treatment of people who have been given particular diagnoses. This can occur particularly in the case of people who have been given a diagnosis of emotionally unstable personality disorder (EUPD), which is sometimes referred to as borderline personality disorder (BPD).

The approach within our county (Gloucestershire) is often to provide only very short-term psychiatric hospital admissions for people who have been given a diagnosis of EUPD. These usually last for a week or two weeks. Clinicians have sometimes expressed a view that they may become 'dependent' on the service if they remain there longer.

Joanna said:

There is a problem with inpatient stays – if people with BPD are lucky enough to be offered one in the first place. Personally, I have been denied a bed on several occasions because 'people with your diagnosis don't do well in hospital'. If they changed the model, there would be no reason that we shouldn't. On the occasions I have been admitted, two of them have been for very short four- to five-day 'respite' stays. These do not work for me. In my opinion, nothing short term works for people with BPD. I don't cope well with change, and it takes me a while to settle in a new environment – by five days I am just about ready to come out of my room for dinner, not to go home.

Individuals adapt very differently to being admitted to psychiatric hospital, and the general rule of short hospital admissions did not allow for Joanna's need for time to adapt to her new environment. She had to be readmitted to the psychiatric hospital shortly after she had been discharged.

Joanna went on to say:

People with BPD need to be taken seriously, our illness needs to be taken as seriously as bipolar or schizophrenia. Respite admissions or even crisis admissions for short periods don't work. People with the aforementioned diagnoses wouldn't be offered only that long – it is just another generalisation.

According to our clients, there also seems to be an emphasis placed on people with a diagnosis of EUPD learning to manage their own crises. If there is such an expectation, then it is important that the service supports and prepares patients to do this, for example by providing specific therapies which can help in the management of self-harm. The National Institute for Health and Care Excellence (NICE 2009) guidelines for BPD describe dialectical behaviour therapy (DBT) as 'an intensive psychological treatment that focuses on enhancing a person's skills in regulating their emotions and behaviour... The therapy can help a person gain control of behaviours such as self-harm.' However, it can be difficult to access such treatments. Clients report having been offered 'DBT skills' instead. These are usually provided by their care coordinator within mental health services, whom they may see once a fortnight. Our clients point out that by providing DBT skills, the 'therapy' part is missing. It is perhaps financial constraints that prevent National Health Service (NHS) Trusts from being able to provide DBT in its full form.

Within Suicide Crisis, we have never applied a specific pathway or approach to working with people who have been given a diagnosis of personality disorder (or any other diagnosis). Our approach is to work with individuals. As a result, the length of time that a person remains under our care is not restricted. The frequency with which clients see us is not restricted. They maintain control over these. On the rare occasions that there do appear to be signs that a person (with any diagnosis) may be becoming dependent on our service, we work with them to reduce the likelihood of this happening. This may mean that greater boundaries of time are introduced, gradually, so that there are increasingly longer periods when they are not in contact with our service. However, we do this in conjunction with the client. We talk it through with them. In addition, we recognise that becoming attached to a member of our team could be exceptionally painful, because the professional relationship will end at some point. On a few occasions, there have been indications that a client is becoming attached to one of our team members. We would never want our clients to experience the pain of loss when that contact ends. In trying to take steps to prevent further attachment (such as a gradual reduction of contact with that team member) we are not seeking to be punitive. We find that clients do understand this. Our actions are not the result of a lack of care – indeed, the opposite. Communication is vital at such a time. I recall that when I explained to one of the clients our concerns that she may be becoming attached to a team member, her response was that she was concerned, too, because the pain of attachment to a member of staff in another organisation had been so intense. She did not want that to happen again, just as we didn't.

My impression is that this kind of collaborative approach to reducing the possibility of dependence is less likely to happen under psychiatric services. Our clients have not reported such conversations taking place. We hear of restrictions and boundaries being imposed on them, particularly if staff feel that they are contacting the service too frequently. Some patients describe being informed that their new care plan will include restricted access to the service: any phone calls made to the crisis team will be time-limited and the content of the calls restricted. The frequency of such calls is also limited. This can feel not only disempowering but punitive, if staff are not working with the patient to reduce contact.

It might seem surprising that dependency on our service happens rarely, even though our care is not time-limited and our clients choose how frequently they see us. Giving clients control over their care appears to have had the opposite effect. In my opinion, it is the fact that we put clients in control as much as possible which helps to prevent them from becoming dependent. Putting clients in control helps to empower them.

CELEBRATING UNIQUE INDIVIDUALS

When a person is deeply depressed, they may find it extremely difficult to recognise their own worth. They may no longer be able to see what they contribute to the world. At such times, it is important to remind them of their unique qualities: the aspects that make them so precious and valued.

When I was under mental health services, I do not recall that clinicians pointed out positive personal qualities in me. The communication was often of a more negative nature. The messages I received were that I was failing, because I was not engaging well with the team or because I was reluctant to take the medication which had been recommended.

At times, it also seemed as if a negative interpretation was placed on aspects of my behaviour. For example, a member of the crisis team described me as 'stubborn'. This appeared to relate partly to my reluctance to take medication. However, I had a profound fear of gaining weight, and weight gain was a side effect of many of the medications. If I gained more than two pounds, I saw this as evidence that the weight increase would become unstoppable. I was attempting to maintain some kind of control after experiencing a profound loss of control during the traumatic event in 2012. The other evidence of my stubbornness was my inability to accept the psychiatrist's decision that I must wait another 18 months for psychological therapy. My strong desire for therapy and persistence in asking for it were not born out of stubbornness, though. They arose from an intense longing for relief from the distressing symptoms of PTSD.

Having accessed my psychiatric records, I note that there are no references to my having any positive personal qualities. However, there are at times references which appear more negative in tone. In one of the entries in my records, a member of the nursing staff in the psychiatric hospital where I was sectioned documented that I was 'aloof'. At the time, I was detained under the Mental Health Act (1983) because I was assessed as being clinically depressed. I recall that I had retreated into my own inner world. I felt disconnected from the people around me and did not have the will nor the energy to talk much. The term 'aloof' usually has negative connotations, and a more neutral description would have been that I appeared 'detached' and communicated very little.

If they had understood the underlying reasons for my behaviour, they would perhaps have used different terms to describe it.

In the midst of a depressive episode, a person may only perceive themselves to possess negative qualities. If they are aware of clinicians forming negative interpretations of their behaviour and actions too, it may serve to reinforce their own feelings in this respect. We need to be so careful about the messages we are giving out to those under our care.

In my opinion, it would be helpful if a patient's positive qualities were placed in a prominent position in their psychiatric records, so that all clinicians who came into contact with them would see them and hold them at the forefront of their mind. This would provide a powerful reminder to staff that the way in which a person behaves when in crisis is not indicative of how they are when they are well. It would help staff to maintain an optimism about patients, which I felt was sometimes lacking during my experiences of mental health services.

I have always felt that the individual qualities that our clients possess are radiantly obvious, even when they are in the midst of crisis or in the darkest depression.

I recall David, one of our clients, telling me that he wished I had encountered him when he was well. He described himself as having a keen sense of humour and being popular because of his ability to make people laugh. In the depths of his depression, he could no longer do that, and felt that he had lost the qualities which had drawn people to him. However, I was privileged to see David at his most vulnerable, open and honest. He shared a part of himself with us that his friends perhaps never saw. The David we saw was deeply caring, sensitive, would never knowingly harm anyone and was courageous in the way he ensured that the interests of those he loved were put first. He was also admirably forgiving towards those who had harmed him.

A client may sometimes find it hard to accept that they possess the qualities that we observe in them and may wonder if we are simply being kind. I know that they may need to hear evidence to substantiate what we are saying. For this reason, it can be helpful to give specific examples of actions they have taken or words they have spoken which provide evidence of the qualities we observe in them.

Many clients believe that their death will be largely unnoticed, because their sense of worth is so low at this point. We need to let them know that they occupy a unique place in the world, they have a unique contribution to make and the world would be different if they were not here. There is no one else like them. We need to see what is unique about them, and celebrate it.

COMMUNICATING CARE NON-VERBALLY

Although I have placed great emphasis on verbal communication, including effective listening, our non-verbal communication can be equally important and just as powerful, particularly in terms of showing the client that we care.

In seeking to maintain professional boundaries, I have felt that a certain amount of caution is needed with regard to touch. Indeed, some people will find any form of touch invasive, and possibly even alarming. We should not assume that a hug or even the encouraging touch of an arm will be welcome.

However, there have been occasions when I have instinctively put my hand on that of a very distressed person or gently touched their arm. On a few occasions, usually when the person is crying so much that they are unable to speak, I have put my arms around them and simply held them.

One night, a female client phoned us to express her intention to end her life that night. We immediately went out to her, and her husband met us at the door. On entering Amy's room, I saw that she was on the bed, crying into a duvet which was covered in vomit. She was highly distressed and unable to speak at that point. She looked so vulnerable and unwell that my instinctive reaction was to put my arms around her and hold her for a few moments. Care and concern can sometimes be expressed so much more quickly and emphatically by a physical gesture.

It was clear that Amy had consumed a very large quantity of alcohol, and we felt that she needed hospital treatment. However, the prospect of this was frightening to her. We spent time talking to her, and after a while she said that she would come to the hospital, if we accompanied her and remained with her while she was being assessed. We were able to build a strong connection with Amy in a very short time. I learned so much about her in the time spent sitting by her hospital bed. At around 4am she was taken from the Accident and Emergency department to a quiet ward, and she settled there. After reassuring her that we would come back later that morning, we left.

Sometimes a client will seek to initiate the physical contact. On one occasion, a male client I had seen at previous appointments asked me to give him a hug. His request was unexpected, and I am usually quite cautious about such physical contact. However, it seemed very important to him at that moment.

I did not realise how profoundly significant that hug was to him, nor what it represented. I knew that his wife had recently left him, and he later revealed that one of the last things she said to him was that his physical appearance disgusted her. He had never lacked confidence in his appearance until then, but now he could not look at himself in a mirror. He even tried to shave without a mirror. He later told us that he had expected us to recoil from touching him. He felt that we would be reluctant to hug him, because he believed himself to be 'repulsive'. Subsequently, he said that our willingness to hold his hand when he became particularly distressed helped in his journey to believing himself to be physically acceptable.

CONNECTING WITH THE FAMILIES OF PEOPLE AT RISK

Although it is not in our remit to support the families of people who are at risk of suicide, it is important that we do. It is immensely distressing and frightening to see your loved one at risk of losing their life. Families often describe feeling very powerless and ill-equipped to help. They are providing love and care in abundance but are often suddenly placed in the role of carer, having no experience or training in how to support someone in mental health crisis. Support for families and carers in such circumstances may be limited. There are times when a family member will phone us or come in to see us because they need to talk through their fears and feelings.

Sometimes clients are introduced to our service by family members or carers. It may be a family member who makes the first contact with us, and it is they who encourage their loved one to see us. In some cases, the family member has a significant amount of contact with us first, and builds a connection with us.

Poppy spoke to us several times before her daughter felt able to come to see us. She was extremely worried that her daughter might be at risk of suicide. While her daughter had not stated this explicitly to her, there had been significant changes in her behaviour, including outbursts of rage and self-isolation, combined with low mood. She told us that her daughter had experienced severe trauma, but was adamant that she did not wish to seek help, primarily because she feared that she would be required to talk about the traumatic event. Perhaps even more significantly, she did not trust anyone enough to feel able to access their help. She did, however, have a trusting relationship with her mother, and her mother had confidence in us. Poppy's daughter respected and trusted her mother's opinion of us, and came to see us. We reassured her that she would not be required to say anything about the trauma which she had experienced and that we only wanted to help and support her. Poppy's daughter came back to see us every week after that. Eventually, she felt able to see a specialist counsellor from another organisation, and we were able to arrange for these appointments to take place at our Crisis Centre.

Calum was also introduced to our services by the person who he now considers to be his mother. Lisa had first met him on a hospital ward, when he was in the bed next to one of her family members. It quickly became apparent to her that he was receiving no visitors, cards or phone calls, and so she made a point of talking to him every time she visited her family member. He slowly began to trust her and was able to talk to her about the events from his childhood which had led to a breakdown in the relationship with his family. Over the months which followed, she and her family met him regularly, and a strong bond developed. He spent more and more time with them, and they ultimately considered him to be part of their family.

Calum had been in hospital because of the physical effects of addiction, and he had spoken frequently of how difficult it had been to access mental health services. Lisa became increasingly concerned about his deteriorating mental health, and at the point she contacted us he was clearly in crisis.

Lisa contacted us days after Calum had gone to a location where he intended to end his life. He had stopped taking the anti-psychotic medication prescribed for him by his general practitioner (GP), and she felt that he urgently needed mental health care. She said that she had been trying to access it on his behalf. After much encouragement from her, he came to see us.

Calum was initially quite guarded and, although he ultimately disclosed a lot of helpful information, he seemed to remain disconnected from us during that first appointment. It took quite some time for him to trust and establish a connection with us. His mother asked him if he would allow us to contact services on his behalf, and he agreed to this. He definitely wanted to access mental health care and rehabilitation for his addictions. He had said at his first appointment with us, 'I wish I could go back to prison, so that I could get mental health help.' He felt that prison was the only place where he could access it.

Lisa always kept Calum informed about the actions we were taking to try to help him to obtain mental health care. She and I were in regular contact. Over time, he came to trust us.

My impression was that Calum had learned to trust people's actions, rather than their words. Ultimately, he engaged extremely well with us. Our relationship with his mother was an important factor in the building of that connection with him.

Lisa told me that she often felt that services perceived her to be a nuisance when she phoned or wrote to them to try to access help or to express her concerns. However, she played such a vital role in Calum's engagement with our service. We need to value family members' input and experience and the detailed knowledge they have of the person at risk.

Some clinicians and services recognise this and actively seek the input of family members and friends, for example when trying to determine a person's diagnosis. Family members most closely involved with the patient may see them far more frequently than clinicians and may have a knowledge of their personal history that spans decades. Psychiatrists may ask to interview family members as part of the assessment process, with the patient's permission, when seeking to clarify diagnosis. This third-party input can be particularly helpful when assessing for mood disorders such as bipolar disorder. Those closest to the patient may have noticed that they experience poles of mood and may be able to recall specific periods of time when these occurred.

Family members and carers can also play a vital role in informing services if their loved one's risk of suicide increases. Sadly, there is evidence that their input is not always heard at such times. In 2017, our charity undertook research (Suicide Crisis 2018) into deaths by suicide in Gloucestershire. Part of this research involved attending inquests. The coroner's court was able to give us information in advance to indicate which inquests we should attend, and in the first six months of our research the coroner found that 25 individuals had died by their own hand. In five out of the 25 cases, the family had warned services in the days before their loved one died that they were at risk of suicide. They were specifically requesting that actions were taken to protect the person, but there was no evidence that their requests had led to any direct action in this regard.

As well as valuing their input, it is so important that we support and protect the mental health of carers. We need to be aware of their possible risk of suicide, as well as that of their loved one. During the first six months of our research into deaths by suicide, we identified a risk of carers developing symptoms of possible serious mental illness and suicidal intent, if they were caring without support. In the cases we studied, the carers had no previous history of mental illness. One of the carers started to develop paranoid thoughts in the weeks before he ended his life. Another started to hear voices. Both were described as being exhausted and overwhelmed by their caring role after a prolonged period of acting as a sole carer, during which time the condition of their loved one deteriorated. Lisa said recently that she feels that her own mental health would have undoubtedly deteriorated had she not been able to phone us at times when she feared for Calum's life or when she felt particularly distressed and overwhelmed. She commented, 'You have walked alongside me throughout this journey.'

As a former carer, I know that it is a privilege to care for the person you love. It is one of the most rewarding and important roles we can undertake. However, there is a need for support for carers to protect their health and wellbeing. Doctors can play an important role in monitoring their mental health and in signposting them to charities specifically for carers, some of which provide counselling and additional services such as peer mentoring.

— CHAPTER 3 —

THE SAFETY NET

Our model of service places a protective net around our clients, and this plays a vital role in ensuring their survival. The safety net is made up of a combination of the Suicide Crisis Centre, home visits and emergency phone lines. This combination ensures that we have more ways of reaching clients, and our clients of reaching us, when they are at immediate risk of suicide. It also ensures that they have more ways to remain connected with us as we provide ongoing support.

Our original plan was only to provide a Suicide Crisis Centre, where clients could visit us. It had not been our intention to provide home visits. However, our first client demonstrated very clearly the need for this additional service. He was referred to us by a psychiatric nurse, who explained that he had experienced something deeply traumatic five weeks earlier. He had been referred for psychological therapy, which at that time had a waiting list of several months. 'He needs to talk to someone now,' she told me. This was our very first client, and I asked her if he would prefer to talk to a man or woman. She simply repeated the same phrase, 'He needs to talk to someone now.'

I phoned him immediately, and it was clear that he was not going to be able to get to our Crisis Centre. He was too traumatised and too frightened to leave the home. After risk assessing the situation, we made a decision to go out to him immediately. We spent an extended period of time with him that afternoon. He said it had been profoundly helpful. When we returned to our Crisis Centre, our team had a discussion and agreed that this was something we would need to provide routinely for our clients, because there would be others who could not reach us. Our first clients helped to shape the services that we now provide.

Some clients for whom we provide home visits have experienced trauma. However, there are many other reasons why a person may become unable to leave the home. A significant percentage of clients seeking to access our service are alcohol or drug dependent, and they may find it increasingly difficult to leave the home as their substance use increases. This was the case for Ellie. Initially, she was able to attend appointments at our Crisis Centre. However, her situation deteriorated rapidly after she attended an alcohol support group meeting within an addiction service.

During the meeting, one of the other group members had disclosed harrowing details of a past trauma. This had triggered memories of Ellie's own traumatic past and she started to experience flashbacks and intrusive memories. Her alcohol intake increased rapidly, as she tried to block out the distressing images that resurfaced in her mind. She was experiencing 'night terrors' – dreams so terrifying and realistic that she would wake believing she was back in the traumatic situation. Her alcohol intake increased to such an extent that it became unsafe for her to go out. She was having regular falls and so she no longer left her home. This meant that she was unable to access treatment or support from the local addiction service. They came to her home a couple of times to try to encourage her to attend appointments at the addiction centre, but they did not have the capacity to provide regular home visits.

Ellie had been having some input from mental health services, but they informed her that they were going to withdraw her care temporarily. They advised her that her mental health care would resume when she had been free of alcohol for a month. They believed that this would be an incentive to stop drinking. They said that they were unable to work with her while she was drinking heavily.

Ellie's situation deteriorated further, and on two occasions when we visited her home, she had sustained injuries as a result of a fall and we had to call the emergency services. She desperately wanted to be admitted to residential rehabilitation but was told that she needed to engage with addiction services in the community first. However, this had become impossible for Ellie.

Our team could not treat Ellie's alcohol addiction nor provide the psychological intervention recommended for PTSD. What we were able to offer was empathy, care, kindness and understanding. Our support was constant and enduring. We continued to visit Ellie during her increasingly frequent hospital admissions to receive treatment for injuries and for her deteriorating physical health.

We continued to visit long after Ellie's suicidal crisis had subsided. There were no other services providing regular support, so it was important that we did.

Sadly, Ellie died of pancreatitis, as a result of long-term alcohol use. I attended her funeral and overheard someone say, 'There are some people who are beyond help.' Ellie was not beyond help. She wanted and needed a type of help that does not appear to exist at present for people who are alcohol dependent, who also have significant mental health issues, and who reach such a point of crisis that they need urgent, intensive care – probably residential care.

If you experience a mental health crisis, it may be possible to be admitted to a psychiatric hospital. It is not necessary to demonstrate engagement with mental health services in the community in order to access it. Indeed, an inability to engage with community mental health services makes it more likely that you will be offered inpatient care. In my opinion, we need a similar level of care for a combined addiction and mental health crisis.

The support that we provided to Ellie in her home took place over a period of months. However, home visits may only be required on a very short-term basis, during a period of crisis. Indeed, one of the most important reasons for providing home visits is that it allows us to go out to clients who are at imminent risk of suicide. A client who is in crisis may be too distressed or too mentally unwell to reach us, and we may need to go out to them immediately. Emergency home visits have been an important part of ensuring that our clients survive. This is one of the reasons why we refer to a 'safety net'. If we did not provide such home visits, there would be gaps through which clients could fall at their time of greatest need.

Providing home visits means that we can cover a wide geographical area and reach clients who might be deterred from travelling to our centres because of distance or lack of access to public transport. Our Suicide Crisis Centres are located in Cheltenham, but much of our work takes place in the city of Gloucester. Indeed, that is where we have seen the greatest demand for our services in the past couple of years. Being mobile also ensures that we can reach the outlying villages and rural areas of Gloucestershire.

We have not only visited clients in their homes, however. At times of immediate risk, I have gone out to clients in various locations, including public parks, rural locations and city centres. On one occasion, a client had been driving to a venue where he intended to end his life and, after talking to me on the phone, he agreed to meet in a nearby supermarket car park. It was the nearest available place to meet, and it mattered that we reached him quickly. I have also gone out to clients in some unexpected locations. Lydia's particular circumstances led to us meeting on a roundabout in the centre of a road.

When Lydia contacted us that evening, it was evident immediately that her presentation was different from usual.

We had been supporting her for several weeks, and she had presented as being low in mood, with suicidal thoughts. This evening, however, her mood appeared to be elevated. Her speech was markedly different. The pace was much faster than usual. I was immediately concerned at this sudden change and, indeed, as we talked on the phone, it became clear that it stemmed from having made a decision to end her life. A person may appear elevated, even euphoric, after such a decision.

The immediate challenge was to locate her and ensure her safety, but it was evident that she was travelling on foot, at first through busy streets and then through a park. I arranged to come out immediately and meet her in the park, but by the time I arrived, she had already left. I was able to make phone contact with her, and she revealed that she was a few streets away. By the time I reached her, she was on a roundabout.

After encouraging her to come with me to a safer location where we could talk, I explained that I was going to need to involve other services because her presentation was so different. Initially she was extremely reluctant. We talked for a considerable period of time before she felt able to accompany me to the out-of-hours service at the local hospital, where she was able to see an on-call doctor, who arranged for the mental health crisis team to assess her that night. It is important that we recognise when it is appropriate to involve psychiatric services. We continued to support Lydia over the weeks that followed.

The more regular, ongoing support of clients may take place in venues other than the home, too. There are times when our first contact with a client is in a general hospital. This is often because a family member or close friend approaches us and asks us to become involved after their loved one has made a suicide attempt. They are quite rightly concerned that they may try to end their life again.

Tammi had sustained catastrophic injuries after her suicide attempt. At my first meeting with her, she explained what had led to her crisis. She had enjoyed considerable success in her professional life for many years, but a series of recent events had affected her reputation. In turn, this had led to her profoundly doubting her abilities. She had no longer felt able to work, and her work had been the focus of her life. There had been subsequent financial problems, and other difficulties.

Tammi had never expected to survive her suicide attempt. At our first meeting, she was still experiencing feelings of shock that she had survived. In the meetings which followed, she began to talk about feelings that she had never been able to disclose to anyone before. She explained that she would not have felt able to share such information with the ward staff or the psychiatric team based in the hospital, because it would have been recorded in her medical records. She was concerned that if she disclosed the depth of her emotional distress about her injuries, and her fears about her ability to live with such injuries, the medical and psychiatric teams would not consider her psychologically ready for the next phase of physical rehabilitation. She also felt the need to give her family the impression that she was coming to terms with her injuries, because she did not wish to cause them anguish or worry. As a result, it was extremely important that she was able to share her fears and feelings with someone who was outside both her family and her medical teams.

We continued to visit Tammi as she progressed through rehabilitation.

There are times when a client may need to be admitted to a psychiatric hospital, and when that happens, we continue to keep in contact with them. As well as visiting them, we let them know that they can phone us if they need to. It is important that we maintain this connection with them, primarily because they may need our support when they return to the community. Sometimes, however, we may in effect provide an additional safety net while they are in the hospital and this can catch them as they risk falling between the gaps created by staff shortages and other circumstances.

I had been visiting Keira in a psychiatric hospital every week, and she told me one day that she was having strong feelings of wanting to escape. I let Keira know that I would need to inform staff of this, and we also explored what might happen if she did leave the hospital. I was concerned that she might not contact other services at this point, and so I encouraged her to call us if she did leave. She said that perhaps she might feel able to do so.

A few weeks later, we received a call from Keira at around 10pm. It was not unusual for her to call at this time. There were fewer staff on duty at night and it was sometimes harder for her to find an available nurse at this time, if she needed to talk.

Initially there was no indication that circumstances were different that night. However, within the space of a couple of minutes, she told me where she was. She had left the hospital and was at a location where she intended to end her life. Indeed, she could have done so within seconds. It is at this point that the trust and connection built previously with the client are so important. Firstly, this was what had enabled her to contact us that night, and secondly, it allowed us to 'hold' her, at a point where she was feeling strong intent to end her life. We were able to talk through what had led to this escalating situation. After exploring this, I explained that I would need to call an emergency service, and she understood the reasons for this. However, while we were waiting for them to arrive, she began to voice concerns that walking out of the hospital and placing herself in a situation of risk would affect her future treatment. She had been hoping to be transferred to a specialist unit for treatment, and an ability to engage and stay safe was a requirement for admission. I explained to her that she had taken active steps to keep herself safe by phoning us, and that she had continually engaged with me during the phone call. I assured her that I would make this very clear to staff at the psychiatric hospital and that I would contact the specialist unit, too, if there was any hint that this incident might jeopardise her place there.

It is important that we can visit and stay in contact with our clients, wherever they are. However, we also need to provide a safe place where clients can come to us. We now have two Crisis Centres. One is in the town centre, which means that it is accessible by public transport from all parts of Gloucestershire. Despite being located off one of the main streets, it is a surprisingly quiet and tranquil venue. The first time I went inside, I felt that it would be a welcoming place for our clients.

However, making their way through the busy streets of a town centre can feel overwhelming for some people, and so we have recently acquired a second Suicide Crisis Centre on the outskirts of town, with open countryside all around. This peaceful location, close to nature, has many benefits. We have access to a garden and are minutes away from fields, which are filled with buttercups in spring and summer. When a client is starting to recover, we sometimes go there for walks.

It was always our plan to provide appointments at our Crisis Centres, rather than a drop-in service. A drop-in service can lead to people waiting, possibly for long periods, and this can be distressing for someone in crisis. They also may not want to be around other people at such times. People in crisis who are admitted to the emergency departments of general hospitals often leave precisely because of the waiting time and the requirement to remain in a busy waiting area with strangers. Providing appointments means that a person can come in and be seen immediately. We have a number of emergency appointments, which means that a person in immediate crisis can access help quickly.

A drop-in service can also deter some high-risk groups of people who we are especially keen to reach. In particular, such a service can deter high-risk men, who are often extremely reluctant to disclose to other people that they are in crisis. Many describe feeling shame and embarrassment. The prospect of being seen by other people in a waiting area would act as a significant deterrent to using our services. If they were seen by someone they knew, news of their suicidal crisis might spread. The prospect of this was alarming to them. It would not only increase their feelings of shame and embarrassment, they told us, but it might ultimately lead to their employer finding out that they were in crisis. They would simply not take that risk.

In addition, we know that some men find it extremely difficult to take the first steps towards seeking help. They may waver in their intent to access it. Time spent waiting can allow time for the fear of what lies ahead to increase, and the sense of acute discomfort to grow. They may walk out without ever being seen.

When John first came to our Crisis Centre, his discomfort was evident. One of my colleagues noticed a man in his middle years, pacing up and down outside. He told us later of the internal conflict he was experiencing during those moments. He said he knew that he desperately needed help, but the prospect of accessing such help was terrifying, and his instinct was to run from it.

My colleague went outside and spoke to him, gently encouraging him to come inside. Even when inside, he told me that he had felt a strong impulse to run. Fortunately, we were ready to see him immediately. We were able to build a strong connection with him during that first appointment.

A drop-in service can also deter some groups of professionals who may have particular concerns about being observed by other people in a waiting area. This can include police officers, who may fear that they would risk meeting someone they had encountered in the course of their work. Police officers are frequently asked to carry out welfare checks if there are concerns that someone is at risk of suicide and are often called out to emergency situations where there is an immediate risk.

Similarly, health care professionals express concerns that they could be recognised by one of their patients who might also be attending our Crisis Centre. We are able to ensure that they are not observed by anyone else, if there is a need for their identity to be kept private.

Health care professionals and police officers also regularly express concerns about the potential impact on their career of having their suicidal crisis documented in their medical records. This may prevent their seeking help from their doctor or from psychiatric services. It is so important that we have independent Suicide Crisis Centres where professionals feel able to seek help.

When clients come to our Suicide Crisis Centre, their appointments usually last for an hour. However, the time is extended if they are at immediate risk. In such circumstances, they may remain with us for a period of several hours. We need to ensure that they stay with us until we feel reassured that they are safe enough to leave.

Providing both Crisis Centres and home visits means that we maximise the opportunities to reach clients in a crisis situation. It also allows us to reach a very diverse range of clients.

Although we always intended to have an emergency phone line for our clients up until 10pm every day, we did not think that we would be able to provide an overnight emergency phone line until we had been operating for a while. Once again, however, a client showed us that we would need to provide that from the beginning.

John came to us in the first week after we opened. He had found it extremely difficult to disclose his risk to anyone. He had already trialled his suicide method, and we considered him to be a high risk case. We felt that he was particularly vulnerable at night, and so we explored what might happen if he felt strong intent to end his life during those hours. He told us that he would not call anyone if he reached that point.

'Would you call us?' I asked. He paused for a moment and replied, 'Yes, I think I might.'

As a result, we immediately put in place an overnight emergency phone line which operates between 10pm and 9am. By using a designated mobile phone for this purpose, we can ensure that the member of staff who is on call has the phone beside them through the night. As I have already explained, John did indeed phone the emergency night number while on his way to a location where he intended to end his life.

It has become a vital part of our service and has undoubtedly contributed to the survival of our clients. On so many occasions, a client has called at the point of suicide or at a location where they could end their life in seconds, as Keira did, shortly after she walked out of the psychiatric hospital.

Clients have not only phoned us on the night emergency line because they have been at risk of suicide. There have also been times when they have felt at risk from someone else.

Maisie had experienced life-threatening domestic violence from a previous partner, and she had been severely traumatised by her experiences. She had not had any contact from him for a couple of years. However, she called us in the early hours one morning, barely able to speak. She was able to let us know that he was outside her home. We requested an emergency police response but he had gone by the time they arrived.

It transpired that he had moved into a property very close to her home. She was able to relocate to another council property quickly, outside the county.

At such times of imminent risk from another person, when a client feels so vulnerable and fearful, their instinct may be to phone us because of the trust already built, rather than the police.

The 'safety net' has played such a vital role in the survival of our clients, and it was effectively designed by our clients themselves. This fundamental part of our service originates from their having shown us exactly what we needed to provide to ensure their survival. Once again, we see the powerful influence of lived experience on our services and how it permeates all aspects of our work.

CHAPTER 4

HOW TO BALANCE PROTECTING CLIENTS WITH GIVING THEM CONTROL

'IT'S YOUR DECISION'

When I was under the care of mental health services, clinicians told me on more than one occasion that it was my choice or my decision to end my life. It was their assessment that I had the mental capacity to do so. Now that I run a Crisis Centre, our clients report having been told the same thing. Many of them are under secondary mental health services and have more enduring mental health diagnoses such as bipolar disorder, personality disorder or schizophrenia.

Perhaps the reason why mental health clinicians use this phrase is that they wish to respect the rights of individuals and give them a sense of greater autonomy. It may also be employed to encourage patients to take responsibility for their actions and discourage dependence on services. It appears to be used sometimes to encourage patients to take greater responsibility for their own survival and to try to avoid an expectation that clinicians will 'save' them.

It is important to examine how patients may interpret this phrase, though, and how it feels to hear it. When I heard it, I felt that it validated the decision to die. It made it appear to be a reasonable, lucid decision which I might have taken after carefully weighing up all the information and evidence available to me. That was not the case, however. My intent to die arose from thought processes that were profoundly altered by my recent experience of trauma. I was not thinking as I usually would. In the case of almost all our clients who have been at imminent risk of suicide, their thinking has been temporarily altered by emotional distress, mental illness or trauma.

I think perhaps if all clinicians understood the potentially catastrophic impact of a traumatic event on a person, they would use the phrase less often. The symptoms of PTSD can feel overwhelming. Flashbacks and intrusive thoughts provide a constant reminder of the event. Even during sleep, you may relive the event on a nightly basis. I felt that I would never escape from it – and that fuelled my suicidal intent.

A person may also experience dissociation as part of their post-traumatic response, and this is not always noticed by clinicians. Dissociation can involve a disconnection between your thoughts, memories, feelings, actions and perceptions. I was fortunate that a psychiatrist identified that I was experiencing a disconnection between my thoughts and emotions, which indicated 'depersonalisation'. He noticed that I would comment on my own emotions and feelings as if I were an outsider observing them. I was detached from them. If you are expressing suicidal intent while you are experiencing this kind of dissociative episode, you may appear calm and in control. The reality is that the emotions you are experiencing are so painful and overwhelming that your mind has unconsciously disconnected from them. Such intense distress is likely to impact on a person's decision making.

A very experienced psychiatrist in an NHS mental health service in another part of the country assessed me and gave his view that my presentation during dissociative episodes risked giving clinicians the impression that I was euthymic (in 'neutral' mood) when I was in fact depressed. This is important because it shows how depressive episodes may not be immediately obvious.

He was not the only psychiatrist to suggest that I was experiencing an underlying depressive illness which had not been immediately apparent to most clinicians who saw me during that period. A depressive illness can affect a person's mental capacity, and that is why it is so important that clinicians recognise it.

According to the Mental Capacity Act, a person is deemed to have the mental capacity to make a decision if they can understand information, retain it, weigh up the information and communicate their decision (Department of Health 2005, Chapter 9, Part 1). Depression can affect your ability to weigh up information. It may alter your thought processes, causing you to believe that there is no hope of recovery from your depressive illness. You may believe that any treatment or therapy offered is pointless, when in reality depression is a treatable illness from which it is possible to recover. Similarly, during a psychotic episode, a person may hear voices which are influencing them to act in a certain way and this impacts on their ability to evaluate information.

I have sometimes wondered whether there is enough focus during mental health assessments on the patient's ability to weigh up information. I was fortunate that I retained the mental capacity to make decisions during most of my time under mental health services. However, at one point I became very unwell and believed that I was receiving messages to end my life on a certain date. I was convinced that if I didn't, there would be far-reaching consequences that would be detrimental to other people. I saw this as part of a much bigger 'plan' with which I must comply. I described myself as being like a cog in a wheel. If I did not comply, the whole plan risked being destabilised. A paramedic was called to assess me and gave his view that I could understand and retain information and therefore his intention was to leave me at home. However, he had not considered the third criterion for assessing mental capacity: the ability to weigh up information. My illness was hampering my ability to do that. Fortunately, another professional was present at the time, and he intervened immediately, detaining me for my own protection. In my opinion, there is a need for far more training on the subject of mental capacity for all clinicians and professionals who encounter people who are at risk of suicide. Furthermore, the very differing views of the two clinicians about my mental capacity show the complexities surrounding this issue, and therefore it is surely best practice not to tell any patient that it is 'their decision' to end their life.

It is not only mental illness that can affect a person's mental capacity. It can be impaired temporarily by high levels of distress, or by drugs or alcohol. On more than one occasion, I have had lengthy discussions with police officers when we have both attended the home of a person at imminent risk. The police officer may argue that the person has mental capacity, while I am arguing that their level of distress means that their capacity is fluctuating, and is at times impaired. My aim at that point would be to ensure that they are taken by the police to the general hospital where they can be assessed by a mental health professional in the emergency department. Police officers have powers to protect people in these circumstances, when mental capacity is in doubt.

When our clients report having been told by mental health services that it is their 'choice' or 'decision' to end their life, they often comment that it made them feel that the clinicians did not care whether they survived or not. This was, of course, not the case, but our clients' interpretation of the phrase highlights the potential risks of using it. It may be interpreted in a very different way from that which you intended. One of our clients said, 'It made me feel they wanted me to do it.' This was deeply concerning to hear.

We need to be tenacious in helping people to stay alive. Within our charity, we actively take steps to hold and help someone who is in suicidal crisis rather than drawing back and giving them autonomy. We do this in all cases, not just when the person lacks the mental capacity to make decisions. This is partly because we care and could not stand back at such a time, and partly because we understand the likely alteration in the person's thought processes at that time – that they are not thinking as they usually would.

Our wish is to do whatever we can to help a person survive. If a client withdraws from us when their risk is increasing, we will take steps to keep in contact with them and let them know that we are concerned about them, that we care and that we remain here for them. And if a client told me that they felt they had reached the end, and had decided to end their life, I would never think, 'Well, that's their decision.'

When I gave oral evidence to the Parliamentary Committee about our work in 2016, I explained that one of our clients had stated an intention to end her life a few days beforehand. She had planned this in advance and had set a date for her suicide. We informed both her GP and our local mental health services as she was also under their care, and they assessed her risks and her mental capacity. The crisis team encouraged her to phone them if she needed to. As the date approached, we were the service actively keeping in contact with her. On the day itself, we knew her planned movements and the final acts she intended to carry out before her suicide attempt. We knew where she was and what she was doing at any given time. Her GP and mental health services were not in contact with her at all in those crucial hours. As I explained to the Parliamentary Committee (8 November 2016, Q176), 'We were the ones who were actively and tenaciously ensuring that she survived.'

There have been times when I have stated explicitly to a client that we would be extremely upset if they died. I have only needed to say this on rare occasions. I have said it at times when a client has been convinced that their death would go unnoticed – that it made no difference to anyone whether they lived or died. They struggled to imagine that anyone else cared about them or valued their existence.

On a few occasions, a client has said to us, 'Please let me go.' They explain that their emotional pain and inner torment are so profound that living has become unbearable. They ask that we withdraw our care and allow them to end their life. At such times, I have to tell them gently that I cannot do that. I cannot leave them to die. This is their hour of greatest need, and my intention is to do all I can at that point to stay connected with them. On every occasion when a client has said this, I have felt they have been deeply depressed at that point, or experiencing such high levels of emotional pain that their thinking is impaired. I have no doubt that the degree of mental suffering they are experiencing is just as they describe it, but I believe that it will not always be as intense as it is at that time. I have hope for them. It is possible that life can improve and be very different in the future, even after immense suffering – or even in the midst of suffering. I know that not all suffering is temporary, and that some may be long term.

When a person is at imminent risk of death because of a physical condition, medical professionals intervene. It should be no different if a person has reached a similar proximity to death because of a mental health crisis. Providing intensive care for someone experiencing profound mental suffering is equally important.

Our approach does not cause clients to place all responsibility for their survival on us. It makes them feel that they are cared for, that they are well supported and that their survival matters to the team supporting them. We give clients a high level of control throughout their experience of our service, and this allows them to retain their autonomy and avoids dependency on us and our service.

BEING IN CONTROL

When I was under psychiatric services, it felt as if I had very little control over the kind of care I received. Clinicians would determine how often I was seen, the kind of care and treatments I received, and when the care ended. This felt disempowering and contributed significantly to my disengagement from services.

After the traumatic experience in 2012, I felt a strong need to be in control, having felt powerless during the event itself. The control placed on me within the psychiatric system was often profoundly distressing.

There is a significant power imbalance between psychiatrist and patient. The psychiatrists are usually viewed as the experts, with the patients the recipients of their expertise. I felt that I had very little input into my own care when I was under mental health services. There were 'professionals' meetings' every few months, which were arranged by the psychiatrists and clinicians involved in my care. The purpose of these meetings was to determine the course of my future care and treatment. The clinicians had discussions, made decisions and created care plans. It was only when I accessed my psychiatric records later that I discovered these professionals' meetings had taken place or that I learned the outcome in terms of the decisions they made. My contribution and views were not part of the process at all.

When I expressed a different opinion from a psychiatrist or tried to have my voice heard, I often felt that it was silenced or unwelcome. When psychiatrists wanted to admit me to a psychiatric hospital, I asked if it was possible to be admitted to a specific ward where I had been before, as this was a familiar place. A psychiatrist commented that I was 'trying to control the situation'. He insisted that I must go to the ward he had selected. However, I had not been trying to seize the control from him. It had felt daunting to go to an unfamiliar ward, where I knew none of the staff. It would have been reassuring, at a time when I was vulnerable and in crisis, to go to a ward where I was known. Even if this had been an attempt on my part to take greater control, I wonder why this was seen as unacceptable by the psychiatrist. It would have been understandable, in the context of the post-traumatic response I was experiencing. It could have been so helpful if clinicians had allowed me to have a greater role in the decision-making process and thereby have greater control over some aspects of my care.

Psychiatrists have power not only over the treatment and care you receive, but also over which diagnosis you receive. The label they place on you will affect the whole course of your future treatment. Some of us actively seek a diagnosis. Harry felt that he had been displaying symptoms of bipolar disorder, but local psychiatrists were unconvinced. During a depressive episode, he attempted suicide and was transferred to a hospital in another part of the country. He was treated there for several months and was eventually diagnosed with bipolar disorder type two. Such a diagnosis can be potentially life-saving, because it allows the person to have access to specific treatments, including mood stabilisers which can help to balance the person's moods. If a diagnosis allows an individual to make sense of the symptoms they have been experiencing, it can be profoundly helpful. It can be the beginning of learning how to manage such symptoms. I know from personal experience that such a diagnosis can significantly improve the quality of a person's life. Since being diagnosed with bipolar disorder, I have been able to develop my own individual coping strategies to help me during depressive episodes, and this has been empowering. A diagnosis can lead you to feel more able to control a condition which you may have previously felt was controlling you.

A diagnosis can help make sense of something which may initially appear inexplicable and terrifying. One of our clients explained that he had feared he was losing his sanity in the weeks after a traumatic experience, until he received a diagnosis of PTSD which helped him to understand what was happening to him. He realised that his bewildering symptoms could be explained in the context of that specific psychiatric condition.

However, if you receive a diagnosis with which you disagree, or which does not seem to accurately describe what you experience, it can be extremely distressing. If you tell the psychiatrist that you disagree with it, they may inform you that you are not 'owning' your diagnosis. How utterly disempowering that may feel. If a client under our care has been given a diagnosis which they feel is inaccurate, I always let them know that they have the right to seek a second opinion. This could take place in another part of the country, if they wanted to ensure that the psychiatrist was wholly independent from the local mental health service. In some cases, this has led to their receiving a different diagnosis.

There is a growing movement to discard the term 'personality disorder'. Many patients reject the term, considering the reference to 'personality' to be inaccurate and inappropriate. One of our clients said, 'It's like saying my personality is flawed. If emotionally unstable personality disorder is about my experiencing intense emotions and sometimes having difficulty regulating them, then why not call it emotional regulation disorder? Why suggest that the core of my personality is intrinsically disordered?' If psychiatrists and clinicians insist on applying the term to a patient, when they object to it and find it profoundly distressing, it can feel extraordinarily disempowering.

Several clients have told us that psychiatrists diagnosed them with a particular condition but did not disclose this to them. All the clinicians involved in their care were party to this information. The patient only discovered the information by accident – sometimes years after the diagnosis had been made. One patient found out from a discharge summary letter from the general hospital. She had been admitted there after a suicide attempt. She discovered from the letter that she had been diagnosed with emotionally unstable personality disorder. None of the mental health professionals involved in her care had told her this. I find this withholding of psychiatric diagnosis particularly concerning in terms of power imbalance.

Throughout their journey under mental health services, patients may be given very little control over their own treatment and care. However, when they experience crisis and state an intention to end their life, they may be told 'it's your decision'. Having been absent from the decisions made about their care up until that point, they are now handed back the power to make a decision about whether or not to end their life. If there is a wish that patients take more responsibility for managing their own crisis, then surely part of the preparation for this should be to allow them to become more involved in decisions about their care at a much earlier stage.

When clients access our services, they determine how often they wish to be seen, the type of care that they will receive and when it will end. Men in particular have told us that they find this level of control over the way they access our services helpful. It can assist in counteracting the feeling of vulnerability which they may experience as a result of seeking help and disclosing that they are in crisis. It can also be extremely important for clients who have experienced traumatic events, particularly where they have experienced a loss of power during that event. They may feel a strong need to be in control afterwards.

Clients can come into our Suicide Crisis Centre every day if they need to. Indeed, many do during the initial stages of their crisis. For most, this lasts for around ten days and then the contact gradually reduces after this. It happens quite naturally. The average amount of time that a client spends with us is a couple of months. Some are with us for a shorter period of time, some slightly more.

Although face-to-face contact forms the most important part of our work, clients may wish to have additional support. They will often show us what this additional support needs to be. We saw this in the case of John, who found that having an email from us waiting for him on his return from work helped alleviate the feelings of loneliness he experienced on arriving at an empty home.

Other men have similarly emailed us between appointments. Oliver started to do this, and we responded. He took the lead, by initiating it in the first place. He had a diagnosis of PTSD, and it became clear that he was exploring aspects of his experience of it in his writing. He would read voraciously and learn as much as he could about the condition and then comment on his findings. Oliver would also write and let us know of strategies he was starting to use. He also emailed at times when things were really difficult for him, and writing provided a powerful means of releasing his emotions. Oliver has been under our services on more than one occasion and always uses a combination of face-to-face support and regular email contact. He has also used our emergency phone lines when he needs to.

Libby was another client who indicated that a different form of support would help her. She told us that she found it difficult to say out loud what she wanted to express, and so she started to send a series of texts, to which we responded. She let us know that she was finding this text support really helpful, and so we continued to provide it for the period that she was under our care.

Some clients may feel initially that they cannot disclose their identity to us because they fear the consequences if they do. It becomes important for them to feel able to decide when they are ready to disclose this. Although we do not provide an anonymous service, we sometimes need to wait for an individual to feel ready to disclose their identity. We adapt to their need. We put them in control of the timing of the disclosure.

I recall that in the case of one man, he would give us neither his name, nor his address or phone number. There were no identifying details at all. We were extremely concerned about his risk of suicide from the information which he disclosed to us over the phone, and we asked him to come to see us that afternoon. We reassured him that we would respect his anonymity and that our priority at this time was to help him. He spent a considerable amount of time with us and appeared to connect well with us. However, he made it clear that he could not give us his phone number nor any contact details. If we phoned him, his wife might answer, he said, and he was adamant that he did not want her or anyone else to know that he was in crisis. He said that he would phone us to make appointments when he needed to. We had never provided this form of anonymous support to anyone before. However, we knew how isolated the man was and that he would have been unlikely to have sought help anywhere else. We felt that we had to adapt to these unusual circumstances in order to help him survive. Effectively, he was able to feel that he was in control of this process by ensuring that only he could contact us and by withholding all identifying information. This continued for a little while, until we had built up trust with him, and then he was able to gradually reveal more personal information and felt comfortable for us to phone him, initially at times when he knew his wife would not be at home.

It is interesting how some clients react when they are told that it is they who will decide when they are ready to leave our service. Initially, they may react with surprise because this is something they may not have experienced under other services. Their surprise is often followed quickly by an expression of relief. Many have told us subsequently that they felt secure and safe, as a result. Once a client responded by saying, 'Well, that's good because I am going to need your care for years.' She thought that at the time, because of the depth of her crisis. However, she didn't need us for years and within a few months she was able to return to work.

There are occasions where a person has more complex needs and they remain under our care for several months. However, the amount of contact always reduces naturally over time. They may ask to see us once a week or once a fortnight by that stage.

Our approach is to give clients as much control over their care as possible, but to actively and tenaciously work to protect them and help them to survive, when they are in crisis and at risk of suicide.

CHAPTER 5

RESPONDING EFFECTIVELY TO CLIENTS IN SEVERE DISTRESS

POST-TRAUMATIC RESPONSES, DISTRESS AND FEAR: SUPPORTING CLIENTS EFFECTIVELY

I have a particular memory of becoming upset towards the end of an appointment with a psychiatrist, when I was under mental health services. This was unusual, as I did not generally express such emotion during my sessions. I had been focusing on some painful memories on that occasion and started to cry. These were memories I usually tried to suppress. Once I had started to release these painful emotions through tears, I seemed unable to stop crying. I recall that the psychiatrist did not react to my expression of emotion, and, within minutes, it was time for the session to end. He told me that he would see me the following week. As I left the room with tears running down my face, I wondered what to do. I would have to walk through a crowded waiting room in order to exit the building, and rather than have my distress observed by other people, I went to the toilets to cry there.

On another occasion, when in a psychiatric hospital, a psychiatric nurse walked into my room and found me crying. She apologised for disturbing me, and then exited the room immediately, informing me that she would come back to talk to me later when I was less distressed. The response of staff was to leave me alone in a room.

This is not the approach we take at our Suicide Crisis Centre. Although generally lasting an hour, a session is prolonged if a client becomes distressed towards the end of it. We wish to be present for them and support them. We are also concerned about their potential suicide risk at such a time and do not want them to leave our Crisis Centre under those circumstances. I fully understand that it might not have been possible for the psychiatrist to prolong the appointment – indeed, perhaps he thought it best to terminate it quickly as it was becoming distressing for me. However, I wondered afterwards why he had not asked if I would like to sit quietly somewhere for ten minutes before leaving. This would have at least provided an acknowledgment of my distress, and would have allowed me to express it in private. If a member of staff had been able to check on me during that time, it would have been even better.

If I found a client crying, in any location or under any circumstances, I would support and comfort them. I would also seek to understand the reasons why they were so upset.

As well as experiencing a lack of reaction from clinicians at times when I expressed such emotion, there were occasions when I felt as if my distress was minimised by staff. When I was in the psychiatric hospital, I experienced a particularly unexpected and severe post-traumatic reaction when a male nurse walked into the room. He looked suddenly familiar, even though I had never met him before this hospital admission. In that moment, I was transported back instantly to the traumatic experience and was reliving it intensely. The nurse who came on duty shortly afterwards had not witnessed my reaction but had been informed of it, and she commented, 'I hear you've had a bit of a moment.' Perhaps the phrase was used in order to seek to normalise my reaction and make it seem less alarming, in retrospect, to the patient. However, it felt quite shocking to me at the time to hear my experience described in this way.

On another occasion, when I was in crisis and having strong suicidal thoughts, a clinician described this as 'having a wobble'.

Although these phrases were no doubt used with good intent, they can make the patient feel that the depth of their emotional response has not been recognised or understood. This is why it matters so much to accurately reflect the person's emotions, to ensure that their feelings are validated. It is also extremely important to clients that they feel that you recognise their potential risk to self and that this is not minimised. Hearing my suicidal crisis described as a 'wobble' made it sound as if my suicide risk had not been recognised and that I was simply experiencing a momentary blip.

It is important to emphasise that there were times when clinicians responded in an extremely helpful way to my distress. On another occasion, I was transported back in my mind to the traumatic event, and this was so terrifying that I could not immediately communicate at all. Indeed, my response was to try to shut out everything around me and cover my face with my hands. I was shaking with fear. The clinician said, 'Tell me what's happening, Joy.' He made efforts to connect with me and asked questions to increase his understanding of what I was experiencing at that moment. On the third occasion when I had this kind of post-traumatic response, the clinician simply said gently, 'You're safe now, Joy.' This effectively re-orientated me to the present time and provided reassurance. On both occasions, I felt that my experience was understood, and I received an empathic response.

Notably, both of those clinicians adopted a gentle approach, and this can be extremely effective when you are trying to connect with someone who is traumatised and at risk. At times when a client may be terrified, gentleness poses no threat to them.

These personal experiences provided me with significant learning which helped to inform my approach to supporting clients who are in distress.

Libby first accessed our services after learning that the man who had assaulted her several years previously was coming up for a parole hearing, which could lead to his release. She was terrified that he would find her again and harm her. After we had been supporting her for a few weeks, she heard from the police that he had indeed been given a date for his release. There were times when Libby sobbed uncontrollably, wracked with fear. When a person feels so intensely vulnerable, distressed and fearful, their instinct may be to withdraw from people. If they are reliving aspects of the past trauma during such an episode of heightened distress, they may perceive any attempt to approach them physically as a threat. However, gentleness may be accepted at such times. They may perceive a gentle tone and manner to be both non-threatening and comforting. Past and present may become confused during such an episode. Gradual re-orientation to the present can be extremely effective. I found the reassuring phrase, 'You're safe now' so effective that I have at times used it to help re-orientate clients. However, the manner of the individual and the way in which they deliver the message is as important as the words.

Gentleness can also be particularly effective in the early stages of building a professional relationship with a client who has experienced something very traumatic. There have been times when a parent has asked us to come and see their son or daughter in such circumstances. I recall that Sophie's mother made contact with us initially. Her mother explained that Sophie had been under the crisis team but had found it alarming whenever an unknown team member arrived at her door. The large number of team members involved in a person's care can mean that total strangers are arriving at your home on a daily basis. Strangers represented a threat to Sophie. It was so destabilising and frightening for her when this happened that she was unable to speak to them. It was the opposite of helpful to her.

The experience had left her reluctant to seek help from any service during her crisis, and as a result her mother was extremely worried about the risk to her life.

Generally, my lived experience is never raised when a new client comes to us, but Sophie's mother had read a recent article I had written. She told me that she was going to let her daughter know that I had lived experience and that I had also struggled to connect with mental health services. She is not the first parent to have done this. I have known other parents adopt a similar approach and have found their son or daughter willing to come to us precisely because of this lived experience. They feel that we will understand the reasons why they have been unable to connect with services, and will have a different approach.

Throughout my interactions with Sophie, I adopted a gentle approach and manner. It was important to speak softly. Loud noise or loud voices were unnerving to her. In terms of building the professional relationship, we went slowly. We went at her pace. Her mother informed us that she felt able to receive an initial phone call, and we ensured that this happened at a time that was comfortable for her. I felt it important that we put her in control of the time of the call. She was able to disclose a lot of very helpful information during that phone call but was not sure whether she was ready to meet yet. Shortly afterwards she sent a text which read: 'Please can I come and see you?' Sophie engaged well during that first appointment and we continued to provide support for her.

It was very important to Sophie that we always sent her a text message a few minutes before phoning her, on the occasions when we needed to contact her in this way. The unexpected was startling to her. The same applied when we had scheduled appointments at her home. We always sent a text just before arriving to let her know that we would soon be there and to reassure her that the person attending was known to her.

I have often wondered why gentleness is not celebrated more. It is rarely one of the qualities that employers specify they are seeking in potential employees. Indeed, I recall that when I spoke of how much I value it in a potential member of our team, someone expressed a concern that it might be 'ineffective'. It is interesting that the word can evoke such negative responses. Perhaps people equate gentleness with a tentative approach. It is the opposite. It can be extraordinarily powerful. It can be life-saving.

There have been times when I have gone out to the home of a client who is at imminent risk and found them with an implement which they could use to end their life. Indeed, on two occasions the client had a weapon in their hand.

We had been particularly concerned about Ethan for several days. He had been distraught after the breakup of his relationship, and we knew that he had a meeting with his ex-wife to finalise some matters on the Friday afternoon. We were keeping in contact with him that day and were prepared to go out to him at short notice. A text arrived from him which did not state an explicit intent to end his life, but there was enough within it to make me concerned and I decided to pay an immediate visit. When I rang the doorbell, there was no response. To my surprise, however, the front door was unlocked and I was able to walk into the house. I said his name as I walked in, and explained that it was Joy. There was only silence. There was no sign of him downstairs, and so I went upstairs, explaining, 'I'm coming upstairs, Ethan. It's Joy.' As I walked into one of the rooms, I could see Ethan standing there with a weapon directed against himself. In such a fragile and unpredictable situation, a gentle approach and manner can be life-saving. It is important to do nothing to startle or alarm the person. There is a need to suppress any shock you feel at that point. I spoke calmly and softly to Ethan. Within the first few minutes of talking to him, I explained that I would need to involve emergency services as well. The trust and connection which you have built with a client plays an important role at such a time. I think Ethan trusted me enough to know that any action I took would have his interests as a priority. I recall that when I phoned 999 for an ambulance, the call handler was understandably concerned about the potential risk to me in this situation as well, where a client had a weapon in his hand. I never felt personally at risk during the incident, however. Indeed, while we were waiting for the ambulance, Ethan said he would not harm himself while I was present. He said he would not have wanted me to witness that.

I knew that the police would also become involved in a 999 incident where a client had a weapon. It would not be permissible to send out an ambulance crew alone to such a situation. For that reason, I said to the call handler, 'Please will you ask the responders to come into the house gently.' Ethan still had the weapon directed against himself, and I was concerned that the sudden arrival of strangers could destabilise the situation. The priority is that the person remains calm and is not startled or unsettled or feels threatened.

When the first responders arrived, they started to come up the stairs noisily and hurriedly. I called to them immediately, 'Please come up gently.' I reassured Ethan that their haste was because they were concerned about him and that he was safe. The police and ambulance crew worked with me to ensure that Ethan felt able to accompany us to the general hospital, where he could recover from the episode and be assessed by a mental health team.

Severe distress does not always manifest itself loudly. I recall the first 20 minutes of a phone call where the person was silent. In such circumstances, it is not immediately clear what the silence represents, but my approach is always to assume this may be a person who is so distressed that they are currently unable to communicate. I spoke from time to time, to reassure them and to confirm that I would remain on the phone to them. Eventually the caller was able to articulate a word. This was the beginning of her engagement with us.

The young woman told us some time afterwards that she had previously called other services, but they had terminated the call after a few minutes. Perhaps they believed it to be a hoax call, or that there was a fault on the line which prevented them from hearing the caller. My approach would be to always assume that it is a genuine call and that there are reasons why the person may not be able to speak initially. If we assume otherwise, we may lose the opportunity to connect with someone who is very much at risk.

RESPONDING TO CLIENTS EXPRESSING INTENSE ANGER

It is not uncommon for a client to express extreme emotional pain through anger. However, anger can provoke strong feelings in the professional supporting them. They may feel affronted by their expression of wrath. This is particularly likely to happen if the client is using swear words. However, the kind of swearing that we hear during these episodes is rarely intended to challenge, criticise or deride the professional. It is an expression of profound distress and pain and often emphasises the loss of control that the person is experiencing at the time. This loss of control is of particular concern when we have already identified that they are at risk of suicide.

In many services, particularly in statutory services, they have introduced 'zero tolerance' policies in which swearing is described as an act of aggression. This may lead to the clinician warning the person that if they continue to use this kind of language, they will terminate the appointment or phone call. I have observed crisis services responding in this way. This can inflame the situation, increasing the person's sense of injustice and anger. It may also cause huge distress and indeed fear, because the person has gone to that service to seek assistance at a time when they feel unable to survive without significant help.

I have noticed several times that clinicians have interpreted what I term 'descriptive swearing' as being directed against them. The patient states, for example, 'This situation is ****** unbearable. I cannot ****** stand it anymore.'

The clinician responds by saying, 'Don't swear at me.' I am surprised how often I hear this. The patient is not directing his language at the clinician. If they were, they would state: 'You are a *******.' This is aimed specifically at the individual and would be categorised as verbal abuse. This is very different from the descriptive swearing we sometimes hear when a client is experiencing high levels of distress and anger.

On several occasions, clients have phoned us after an incident has triggered intense feelings of rage. In our experience, clients rarely swear during appointments, and, if they do, they often apologise for having done so. When a client is swearing profusely during an episode of rage, this marks a significant change of behaviour. They are less able to control what they are saying and therefore may be less able to control their subsequent actions. It is a signal to me that we need to be particularly concerned about their risk. Indeed, they often state explicitly that they are having strong thoughts of suicide at the same time.

At this point, my entire focus is on helping the person to survive. It is important to allow the person to ventilate their anger to enable them to return to a calmer state. We try to understand what has caused their anger. We validate their emotion. In every case I have been able to understand why the person has experienced such intense rage.

It is better that we let the person express their anger at this point rather than asking or expecting them to suppress it. If they are not able to express it outwardly, they may turn it inwards and act violently towards themselves.

Those of us who are privileged to work with people who are in crisis should be prepared for the fact that they may behave in a very different way from usual and that they may be in a highly charged emotional state. Our focus should be on them, rather than on how their anger or heightened emotion makes us feel. Of course, we need to ensure our own safety at such times, and the safety of others. To place this in context, though, I have been running a Suicide Crisis Centre for five years and neither I nor any of our team have felt at risk from a client during this period. The potential emotional impact on us of witnessing such distress does need to be acknowledged, however, and this would be explored during debriefing or supervision afterwards.

Our response to our clients in these situations may make the difference between their engaging with us or disengaging completely. If their anger is criticised or deemed inappropriate, they may leave the emergency department or walk out of the appointment with their clinician or end their call to the crisis line. They may be doing so at a time when their life is at risk. Our focus must be on them. We need to do all that we can to ensure that they continue to engage with us and that we remain able to help them through their crisis. We need to react in a supportive way to their anger.

Anger is a justifiable and understandable response to many situations, and this is another reason why I become concerned when professionals react negatively to it. We have supported a number of clients who have disclosed that they were sexually assaulted in the past, and who express intense anger during appointments. It is important to acknowledge the justification of their anger. In threatening to terminate a call or end an appointment with an angry client, a clinician risks giving them the message that anger is unacceptable.

We should take reassurance from manifestations of emotion which can be so harmful to the individual if internalised.

Despite welcoming expressions of emotion, I recall an occasion when a client's rage impacted on me to such an extent that it was a challenge to remain wholly focused on her in those moments. It was her first session with us. She initially seemed to engage well but then seemed to withdraw. Towards the end of the appointment she said, 'You have the same diagnosis as that vile man on television, don't you?' It transpired that she had read an article about my diagnosis of bipolar disorder shortly before coming to her appointment. She became extremely angry, informing me that a person with my diagnosis had attempted to murder her in the past. This was particularly hard to hear as I had only been diagnosed fairly recently. I was still coming to terms with how I felt about having the disorder. In those moments, I became painfully aware that some people will make negative assumptions, some may fear me and some may associate my diagnosis with violence and criminality. Despite experiencing strong feelings in response to her words, it was important to refocus on the client and acknowledge the horrendous trauma of the attack she had experienced. It is absolutely possible to understand that such a trauma could lead to anger against a specific group of people, particularly if the person has not been supported or provided with any therapy or assistance to process what happened to them.

CHAPTER 6

ASSESSING RISK ACCURATELY

Our ability to assess risk accurately is vital and is the result of a combination of factors which include our formal training in risk assessing, our knowledge of the client, attention to detail, and the consideration of all relevant information.

FORMAL TRAINING IN ASSESSING RISK

In assessing risk, we are not only considering the person's current presentation but also the impact of past events and known future events that are likely to affect them. In our research into deaths by suicide in Gloucestershire in 2017 (Suicide Crisis 2018), we came across evidence that clinicians had apparently not taken into account all such relevant information, and this led them to underestimate the person's risk of suicide. This was apparent in 24 per cent of deaths by suicide in our county between June and December 2017.

In some cases, individuals were assessed as being at low risk of suicide by mental health professionals a few days before they died, despite the person having made a suicide attempt in the hours before that assessment and despite the apparent presence of other significant risk factors.

Shane was one of the individuals whose inquest took place during the second half of 2017. As well as attending his inquest, we spoke to his family on several occasions and learned about Shane from them. Families who felt able to talk to us contributed significantly to our research. Shane's mother shared with us information from his psychiatric records, as well as the witness statements provided to the coroner by psychiatrists, clinicians and other professionals involved in his care.

Shane was assessed as being at low risk of suicide by a mental health professional in the general hospital a few days before he died. He had been admitted to hospital after making a suicide attempt the previous day. From the information in his psychiatric records and the evidence given by mental health professionals at inquest, we identified the following risk factors:

- Recent suicide attempts.

- A history of self-harm.

- An assessment by a hospital doctor as 'suicidal' the day before the other assessment.

- A diagnosis of borderline personality disorder and antisocial personality disorder.

- Apparently no access to NICE-recommended therapies, which can help with the symptoms of BPD and antisocial personality disorder.

- Drugs and alcohol use.

- A history of offending behaviour.

- A traumatic experience in early adulthood, apparently untreated with psychological therapy. His mother felt that this continued to have a severe impact on him.

- Fear of an imminent prison sentence.

- Fear of abandonment – he had concerns that his mother was about to emigrate.

- Difficulty engaging with services.

- An imminent change in care setting. Shane was about to move to new supported housing, and he had a history of crisis and self-harm whenever he had to make a move like this.

This shows the importance of taking into account a person's history and any known future events likely to impact on risk, such as a change of care setting or possible prison sentence. The combination of all these risk factors would not have led us to assess Shane as being at low risk of suicide, however he was presenting on the day.

It appeared that some clinicians were too heavily influenced by the person's presentation at the time of assessment. If a person stated that they felt better at that point, professionals often felt reassured. In such circumstances, we should be cautious for several reasons. There are of course multiple reasons why an individual may seek to minimise their risk when in the presence of a mental health or other professional. They may have strong intent to end their life, and they may fear that such a disclosure would cause clinicians to intervene and prevent that, perhaps by detaining them under the Mental Health Act (1983). However, it is also possible that a person can start to feel a little better when they are in the highly supportive setting of a general hospital, surrounded by caring and attentive staff. The same can apply when they are at a Crisis Centre, or in the presence of a professional with whom they feel safe and reassured. Their feelings may change when they return home, particularly if they live alone. Their situation can then deteriorate very rapidly.

For this reason, we always take a cautious approach in a situation when a client has attempted suicide, whatever they are saying afterwards. We support them intensively in the days afterwards, even if they initially say that they are feeling better. They are highly vulnerable at such a time. This is especially the case if they have taken an overdose of medication. The body is likely to be in chaos in the days that follow. They have effectively poisoned themselves. This internal chaos can impact significantly on a person's mental and emotional state, particularly in the first ten days after the attempt.

Even if someone is expressing regret or remorse after a suicide attempt, this should not necessarily reassure us. Our research showed that regret after a suicide attempt did not always prevent a further suicide attempt shortly afterwards.

It would be beneficial if crisis services took the approach of routinely providing support after a suicide attempt – ideally the kind of intensive, daily support that we would provide in such circumstances. We found so many instances in our research where a person made a suicide attempt but was provided with no follow-up or care in the days afterwards.

KNOWLEDGE OF THE CLIENT

In Shane's case, the mental health clinician's lack of previous contact with him may have contributed significantly to her assessment that he was at 'low risk' of suicide. There was no evidence that she had met him before. There may be limited time for a clinician to read through a patient's previous psychiatric notes.

The in-depth knowledge we have of clients under our care is extremely important when assessing their suicide risk. It allows us to notice subtle changes in behaviour which may be indicative of increased risk. We are also able to notice small changes in body language or tone of voice. It is not unknown for the most scrupulously honest person to try to withhold the fact that they have an intent to end their life imminently. When people are trying to conceal the truth, it may be detectable from a change in their tone of voice or body language. If you have had a considerable amount of contact with the person, you are more likely to recognise such changes. I am particularly sensitive to changes in voice tone. I trained to teach English as a second language in the past. As many of our students were beginners and spoke no English at all, we were trained to read body language and listen intently to voice tone.

Pete was another young man whose inquest took place in 2017, and we studied his case as part of our research. Pete had revealed vital information through his body language shortly before he died, his family told us. He was assessed by a clinician the day after he had gone missing and had left a suicide note. The clinician came out to see him and concluded that he was 'not suicidal'. Pete's father questioned this as he was extremely worried about his suicide risk. Later his family asked the clinician if Pete had been covering his mouth during the assessment, and he confirmed that this was the case – he had been using his top to do so. 'Pete does that when he is not telling the truth,' his family explained. If the clinician had known Pete, it is more likely that he would have noticed this change in body language.

Pete's case shows the importance of attention to detail and a focus on the non-verbal signals people give out. We need to take into consideration all the ways in which a client is communicating information to us, even if this is not being done consciously.

Pete's case also shows the importance of the information that family members can provide. It is understandable that the clinician wished to see Pete alone. A person may feel able to talk more freely if family members are not present. However, those closest to the person will have observed their behaviour in recent days and weeks and can provide information that the clinician may not be aware of. Perhaps if clinicians invited family members to join their loved one in the last five or ten minutes of an assessment, it would enable them to share their observations about the person's risk. This would also have allowed Pete's family to draw attention to the concealing of his mouth, and what this signified.

Certainly, if a family member or close friend contacts a service to provide information in relation to a person's suicide risk, it should be acted on. We should listen intently and welcome the fact that it is being provided. In our research, however, we noted that in one in five of the deaths by suicide, family members had contacted services in the days before the person's death to express concerns about their suicide risk. They frequently expressed in their evidence at inquest that they felt their input had not been heard or acted on.

If a client is not known to us, then there is even more reason to err on the side of caution when assessing their immediate risk. Our research looked at the case of a man who attended the general hospital after a suicide attempt and was assessed by a mental health professional. He had never had contact with mental health services before and was entirely unknown to them. He reassured them that he would stay safe and as a result, no follow-up care was put in place. He died by suicide a few days later.

There is no doubt that the strong relationship we build with our clients makes a difference to our ability to accurately assess their risk. This trusting relationship encourages disclosure on the part of the client. It can be difficult for a person to withhold the truth about their suicidal intent when an organisation and its individual workers have devoted so much time to helping them to stay alive. We have found that withholding information about their suicide risk does not sit easily with our clients. They tend to speak in terms of 'I couldn't *not* tell you'. As John said, 'I couldn't have ended my life without talking to you first. You have done so much for me.'

Knowledge of the client is important in detecting changes in behaviour. I have already referred to the impact of a sudden outburst of rage on imminent suicide risk. However, we may also notice that a client is repeatedly displaying higher levels of anger over a longer period of time, when such behaviour was not evident previously. I observed this in the case of Anthony.

We had supported him in the past and had not known him to display anger before, but he was now describing episodes where he expressed rage to hospital clinicians or staff at his GP surgery. He had recently become a carer for a member of his family, and it appeared to me that he was experiencing significant stress as a result but was receiving no support in his new role. My concern was that he was becoming increasingly exhausted and feeling overwhelmed, and I felt that his expressions of anger were in part the consequence of a build-up of stress and utter exhaustion.

The condition of Anthony's family member was deteriorating rapidly. He was experiencing emotional pain and fear in relation to this, as well as a feeling of powerlessness to prevent his loved one's further physical decline. His outbursts of anger may have been a way in which he was inadvertently releasing these painful emotions. His higher levels of anger over a prolonged period made me more concerned about his suicide risk, however. He was also becoming more isolated as a result of his anger. He described having arguments and falling out with friends whom he had known for years. With Anthony's consent, I contacted his GP, a local counselling service and a local carers charity to request additional support for him.

Attention to detail is vital when assessing a person's risk of suicide. I know this from my own experience of being a patient. When I read my psychiatric records, I found that clinicians had inaccurately noted information about my appearance on some occasions. At times, this influenced their assessment of my suicide risk. It is documented on one occasion that a member of the crisis team had called round to see me. She rang the doorbell, but I failed to answer the door. Shortly afterwards, she observed that I left my home. She recorded that I was 'wearing makeup and dressed for a night out'. This was, however, not the case. Firstly, I was not wearing makeup. The only time I wear makeup is when I am speaking at a conference or some other public event. Secondly, I was dressed in a top and skirt, which was regular attire for me. I am not sure why that signalled 'a night out', but that presumption led the crisis team member to assume that they should not be concerned about me, and therefore they made no attempt to approach me or speak to me to assess my risk of suicide. Neither did the crisis team attempt to contact me again that evening. In reality, I had suicidal intent that evening and my leaving the home was in relation to that.

There were other occasions when physical detail was recorded inaccurately in my records. One clinician regularly documented that I was 'casually dressed in top and trousers'. I never wore trousers in the summer. Although this repeated error was not in itself of huge significance, it made me wonder what other detail they might have failed to notice and what else they might be recording inaccurately.

The crisis team member made a massive assumption in assessing my appearance as indicative that I was dressed up for a night out. Even if a person is wearing makeup and is well dressed, we should be careful of the interpretation which we place on this. I would not assume that a person who had taken great care over their appearance was necessarily at any less risk of suicide. We are right to be concerned if a person starts taking less care of their appearance as this may be a sign of depression. However, this should not lead us to be automatically reassured if the person in front of us is smartly dressed.

Professionals are often highly attuned to changes in a person's mood which may indicate a depressive episode. However, our research into deaths by suicide showed that not all clinicians appeared to recognise that if a person is presenting as brighter in mood after a period of depression, this can be an indication of increased risk. The clinicians took the apparent improvement in mood as evidence that the person was starting to recover from the period of depression. They were reassured by it. This apparent improvement in mood was documented in the case of several patients at their last appointment before their death.

When a person's mood starts to improve a little, they may gain the necessary energy needed to end their life, which was lacking when they were deeply depressed. A brighter mood can also be an indication that a person has made a decision to end their life. A doctor asked me recently how he and his colleagues could possibly tell if the brighter mood signified the early stages of recovery or that the patient was at greater risk. My advice was that they should continue to support and monitor the person as closely as they did when they were deeply depressed. Additionally, if the person's mood is heightened so much that they appear elated, then this should be taken as a potential sign of immediate risk and a mental health professional should be asked to make an urgent assessment.

One of the more worrying misconceptions in relation to suicide risk is that if a person is seeking help, then the risk is low: 'A patient who is genuinely suicidal will not seek help.' A very high proportion of people who go on to end their life seek help at some point. They may be asking for help at that moment, but later the same day, tomorrow or next week their distress or despair may increase and they may reach a point where they no longer seek help. We may only have this small window of opportunity to help them. It is our opportunity to engage them and encourage them to continue to connect with us in the coming days and weeks.

Our research into deaths by suicide showed that sometimes knowledge of a client's history can lead to clinicians making unhelpful assumptions about a person's current risk. The patient's history is of vital importance, but we also have to reassess each new crisis as it occurs. In the case of one young man, it stated on his care plan that his risk of suicide was low. The psychiatrist responsible for his care stated at his inquest, 'He always kept himself safe.'

Each time a person presents to us, I know that their level of risk may differ from that observed on previous occasions. The fact that a person has always 'kept themselves safe' up until now does not mean that we can rely on this always being the case. This may be the day when that changes.

The coroner decided that the circumstances of the young man's death did not meet the criteria for an Article 2 inquest, which is a more in-depth investigation. Article 2 of the European Convention on Human Rights (Council of Europe 2010) ensures that there is a duty on the part of the state to protect life. It is triggered at an inquest if it appears that there was a real and immediate risk to the life of an individual but that an 'agent of the state' may have failed to take appropriate measures to protect their life. An agent of the state may include a statutory health service, local authority or the police.

In the case of the young man, the coroner decided at the pre-inquest review that Article 2 was not triggered, after hearing the submissions provided by lawyers representing the local mental health service, police and other emergency services. Although the young man had contacted several statutory services to state a clear intention to end his life that night, lawyers informed the coroner that he regularly did so. The coroner's decision concerned me because it could be interpreted as suggesting that if a person is regularly stating an intention to end their life, then the risk is perceived to be less real or that the state has less responsibility to protect their life, perhaps because they could not be expected to know that the risk was real. At our Suicide Crisis Centre, our team has to assume that each time a person states suicidal intent, there is a real and immediate risk and we act accordingly. It does not matter how many times they have done so previously.

The care plan devised by mental health services focused on the young man taking personal responsibility. Earlier on the evening of his death, he had harmed himself. He informed emergency services that 'it's spurting – it's bleeding lots'. The call handler acted according to the care plan, which all statutory services involved in his care had agreed. She asked him to go home and manage his wounds. However, the ambulance service representative stated at inquest that they recognised the need to 'make a clinical decision based on each incident' and that the care plan was for guidance, rather than being prescriptive. The young man made several calls to emergency services that evening. During the final phone conversation, the call handler recognised that something was 'different'. Initially, when he stated an intent to end his life, she suggested once again that he went home. He said he was hearing voices telling him to end his life. The call handler replied, 'I'm telling you to go home.' However, she then identified a change in presentation, 'He just kept repeating over and over again that he would do it. He was so insistent.' This was what she identified as different, and an emergency ambulance was dispatched at this point, but the crew was unable to locate him. It is believed that he died a few minutes after that final phone conversation.

The young man's case has continued to trouble me, for multiple reasons. It was equally troubling to the lawyers I contacted, when I sought their opinion and advice. Among their concerns was the fact that it had not been designated an Article 2 inquest.

We should be cautious about presuming that a person's previous presentation during a crisis will necessarily be indicative of their future presentation. Sometimes clients will contact us immediately after phoning mental health services, because they feel such assumptions were made. If they have experienced a suicidal crisis previously, they sometimes report that they were asked by the clinician on the end of the phone, 'What did you do last time you felt like this?' The client will often have replied, 'I haven't felt like this before.' The clinician's intention may have been to encourage the person to draw on their own inner resources or coping strategies at that point. However, many people find it hard to relate their current crisis to any other. The circumstances may be entirely different. The thoughts and emotions they are experiencing may be different. This is why we need to look at each new crisis with fresh eyes. It is important to explore with the client the circumstances of this new crisis and really understand its impact on them. It is vital to acknowledge that each crisis is likely to be different and distinct from others. In assessing risk, we need to be aware of the client's history and the possible impact of known future events, but we must also be highly alert to their current presentation and circumstances as well, and in particular how these may differ from what we may have observed before.

Sometimes there may be a sudden and unanticipated increase in a person's suicide risk, as a result of a triggering incident or for some other reason.

Luke describes how he woke up one particular morning feeling fine. He had recovered well from his suicidal crisis two years previously and had not been having any thoughts of ending his life. He spent the day looking after his grandson. Sadly, his health had deteriorated in recent months and he had been forced to give up work, which had left him struggling financially. He was unable to afford to buy his grandson the things he wanted that day, not even an ice cream: 'An ice cream doesn't cost much, grandad.' When he spoke to us on the phone later, he described how this had left him feeling deeply inadequate as a grandfather. He was unable to provide financially for him. He felt that this had caused him suddenly to reconnect with the deep sense of inadequacy which had contributed to his suicidal crisis two years previously, when his wife left him. He had felt unable to provide for her physical needs.

Despite having woken up feeling 'fine' that morning, he said he found himself later that day at a location where he intended to end his life. Afterwards he was shocked and frightened at how rapidly this situation had escalated.

Although we can look at Luke's situation and see that there were a number of factors which meant that there was an ongoing medium risk of suicide, and an increased vulnerability at that time, the sudden escalation to being at high risk on that particular day was unanticipated. What was important in this situation was that Luke felt able to disclose his risk of suicide and seek help. He cited the connection and trust that he had built with us two years previously as the reason for doing so.

CHAPTER 7

MEN AND SUICIDE

It is known that men may find it more difficult to seek help when they are in crisis. However, a high proportion of our clients are men – consistently more than 50 per cent and in some weeks as high as 80 per cent. We did not expect to see such a high proportion of male clients, and so we have sought to determine why they felt able to access help from our service, particularly as many of them had stated that they would not have approached other services. Some of the reasons they gave have been explored in previous chapters and are therefore only referred to briefly here.

CONFIDENTIALITY

The confidentiality of our service was cited as an important factor. Some male clients said that they would not have felt able to disclose their thoughts of suicide to a doctor or mental health clinician, because it would have been documented in their medical records. They feared it might impact on their current or future employment prospects. They cited this much more frequently than a fear that disclosing their risk to a doctor would lead to their being detained under the Mental Health Act (1983). Concerns about the impact on their employment prospects were expressed by men who were in a wide range of different jobs, including health care professions, the police force, security positions and professional drivers (a group which includes pilots, train and coach drivers, and drivers of taxis and heavy goods vehicles).

We do not routinely inform a client's doctor that they are using our services. When I gave oral evidence about our Suicide Crisis Centre to the Parliamentary Committee which was undertaking an inquiry into the measures needed to prevent suicide (Health Select Committee 8 November 2016), some of the Members of Parliament felt that we should routinely inform the client's doctor when they first accessed our service. They felt that the doctor should always be at the centre of a person's care. However, this would deter many high-risk clients from coming to us. If we wish to reach men who are off the radar of other services – the ones who are least likely to seek help from anyone – then it is important to recognise that a policy of routine disclosure to a doctor could be a deterrent.

Some services for people in crisis are run by charities but operate by referral from a doctor or health professional in the first instance. I feel it is important that people are able to self-refer, because they may feel unable to disclose their risk to a doctor or health professional, not just because of concerns about the impact on their employment prospects.

DIFFICULTIES IN DISCLOSING TO A DOCTOR OR HEALTH PROFESSIONAL

Some men also cited 'pride' or the need to appear 'strong' or 'in control' as a reason for not disclosing their suicidal thoughts to their doctor. It is well documented that men often feel pressure to present as 'fine' to their friends and colleagues. It is perhaps less well known that they may feel a similar pressure to appear as such to their doctor. Despite being a professional rather than a peer, a doctor is still someone to whom they are 'known', someone they may have to encounter again in the future. There was a reluctance to disclose information about their crisis to anyone who knew them.

They may never have been emotionally vulnerable in front of their doctor before. Additionally, the reasons behind a man's suicidal crisis may touch on deeply personal matters of a sensitive nature, which they struggle to disclose to anyone. As one of our male clients explained, 'If I had told my doctor that I was feeling suicidal, I would have had to explain why, and I couldn't tell him that.'

Luke's wife had left him two months before he came to our Suicide Crisis Centre. In an angry exchange in the minutes before she walked out, she had criticised his appearance and his sexual performance, citing these as reasons for ending the marriage. When he told his doctor that his wife had left him, the doctor reassured Luke that he had been a good husband and father, and that he was a good man. Luke told us:

> I felt ashamed to be called a man. I felt inadequate and so full of shame for not being 'manly' enough. I felt like a shamed, lost little boy. I felt I wasn't a man at all. How could I tell my doctor, who believed me to be a good husband and father and a good man?

Luke told us that he could have spoken to his doctor about the most intimate and embarrassing physical health problem, but he could not tell him the things that his wife had said to him on leaving him for another man.

Some of our male clients have said that they wanted to tell their doctor, but struggled to do so. I recall phoning a doctor to let him know that one of his patients, who had visited our Crisis Centre that afternoon, was having suicidal thoughts. Joshua had attended an appointment with his doctor that morning, with the intention of disclosing his suicidal thoughts, but had found himself unable to do so. He had talked about a physical health issue instead. Joshua needed to build up to telling his doctor and the ten-minute appointment, which is the norm at doctors' surgeries here, gave little time for that. It felt too pressurised. He told us that it had taken him several hours of building up to phoning us that afternoon before he was finally able to do so.

When I told Joshua's doctor about his suicidal thoughts, he replied, 'He seemed fine this morning.' He seemed to doubt that it was possible that the young man he had seen earlier that day could be having these thoughts.

From an early age, many of us become adept at presenting as though we are 'fine' when extremely distressing events are happening in our lives. We may have to continue to study or work during such times and so we develop an ability to put on a professional front when the most deeply painful events are taking place in our personal lives. We feel under an obligation to be able to function well at work, and to appear to be coping. This can extend to appearing fine to friends and family, too, if we choose not to disclose, or feel unable to disclose, the personal anguish that we are experiencing.

This may explain why some of us are also able to appear 'fine' when having suicidal thoughts. We may have become skilled at covering up pain. We may have learned to do so throughout our adult life.

NOT A DROP-IN SERVICE

Many of our male clients stated that they would not have felt able to walk into a drop-in crisis centre – the kind of centre where people can turn up without an appointment and wait for a member of staff to see them. This would usually require waiting in a communal area with other people. As I have explained previously, many of the men we see do not want other people to know that they are in crisis. They are concerned about being observed walking into a drop-in centre or encountering someone they know there. It is important to them that only our team is aware that they are accessing our service.

If they had been obliged to sit in a waiting room or communal area with other people who were attending the

Centre, they felt that this may also have led to other clients attempting to converse with them, and this would have felt exceptionally uncomfortable to them at a time of crisis, they said.

Our male clients want to know that they can come into our Crisis Centre and be seen immediately, thus limiting the likelihood of being observed by other people. An appointment-based service is therefore important to them.

Our Crisis Centres are not identified as such from the outside, and we do not routinely disclose their location unless someone needs to access them. This means that it is not apparent to a passing member of the general public why someone is walking into the building.

FLEXIBILITY OF ACCESS

Clients usually access our service initially by phone and then arrange to come in to see us. However, if this was the only route to our services, it would have deterred some men. It can be extremely difficult for them to seek help. They may never have done so before. Picking up the phone and then walking into a Crisis Centre may appear too big a step, and they may need to take more tentative steps to seeking help. They may send a brief text message or short email instead. These are often exploratory communications. They are 'testing the water' initially via this written contact, to see how it feels to be in communication with us and what kind of response they receive. It may also be easier to express in writing how they feel rather than voicing it out loud. Over a period of a few days, this email or text contact may continue and they start to build trust with us through these communications. Only then will they feel ready to start face-to-face support.

The men who contact us in this way are not seeking an anonymous text or email service. These are the first steps in connecting with and becoming known to a team who will build a trusting, supportive relationship with them via face-to-face contact.

John initially sent us a succinct three-line email which explained that his wife had left him and that he was having thoughts of ending his life. Over the three days which followed, we exchanged a number of emails. This allowed John to build trust with us and start to feel a connection. He then felt able to come in to see us. As I have already described though, he still found it extremely difficult to walk into our Crisis Centre, and paced up and down for some time outside before a member of staff encouraged him to come in. It's important that service providers realise how exceptionally difficult it can be for some men to take the step of seeking help and therefore we should provide as many routes as possible to facilitate their access to a service.

CONTROL

The fact that we place clients in control of their care as much as possible is important, men tell us. They can decide how often they wish to see us, the kind of support they receive and when they feel ready to leave.

There are times when we may need to take more control, however: for example, if the client becomes more mentally unwell or if they are at immediate risk. At such times, we have to protect them. Additionally, if a client is in emotional turmoil when they first come to see us, they may struggle to know how often they would like to see us or what kind of support would be helpful. Jack pointed out that when he was deep in crisis, he willingly placed more of the control in our hands, 'I was confused, distraught, heartbroken, dazed, bewildered, panic-stricken and felt totally to blame for everything.' He vividly describes the combination of shock, confusion, fear, guilt and emotional pain which he was experiencing. He had endured such inner turmoil in those first few days that it was difficult for him to make any decisions about his care. 'I think I felt you took control at that point, and I felt very comfortable with that,' he said.

Jack explained further:

> In those early days, in the depths of my crisis, I looked for your support and guidance to steer me out of the darkness. My traumatic experience left me feeling blind and unable to move forward without you taking my hand, steadying me and leading me forward. Then eventually I felt able to let go and walk beside you. Finally, you enabled me to walk on ahead of you towards recovery.

We offer control to the client but recognise that there may be reasons, as in Jack's case, why they are not yet in a place to be able to take it. Offering control to the client is different from expecting that they should be ready to take it.

I feel that we should be particularly cautious about expecting that the patient should necessarily be in a position to 'take responsibility' for their care. Our local mental health service has a psychological therapies service for people who are experiencing depression or anxiety. I was surprised to hear from clinicians working within that service that their usual policy would be to routinely discharge a patient who missed two appointments in a row, even if they had not been able to determine why the person had not attended the sessions. Some of our clients report having been discharged under these circumstances. I am told that the view is that the patient has responsibility for attending (and presumably for informing the service if they cannot attend). Clients of ours received letters informing them that they had been discharged. The service had not been aware of the reasons they had not attended.

The psychological therapies service is aimed in particular at patients who are clinically depressed. If their depression becomes more severe, they might struggle to attend appointments. Depression is an illness which may profoundly affect a person's ability to function. I feel it is important that services are willing to be proactive and that they are prepared to take over some of the responsibility when a person is unwell or in crisis. I would wish to do all I can to find out why the person is not attending – and to explore what we could do to help them to continue to engage. Our clients (who had been discharged) reported that a deterioration in their mental health had prevented them from attending the psychological therapy appointments.

SMALL TEAM

Men have told us that they prefer to be supported by a very small team. Usually only two members of staff are involved in their care. However, we have noted that some men have only felt able to be supported by one member of staff – the first person who assesses them.

In accessing our services, our male clients take the hugely courageous step of expressing their deep emotional pain, their distress and their fears to another person. This may be something they have never revealed to anyone before. They may only feel able to do this once. They may only feel able to show this level of vulnerability to one person. More than one male client has told us that if they had been passed to another member of the team for subsequent appointments, they would not have returned. This only applies to a small percentage of our male clients but it is usually those who are at the highest risk.

Luke explained to me why the circumstances of his wife leaving him meant that he only felt able to disclose this information to one team member:

For me, I suppose, the barrier in being able to talk to anyone was because she left me for the following reasons. She told me that she was in love with another man who satisfied her physically. That when I touched her, I made her skin crawl. That I was fat and ugly and always ill and that she wasn't my carer. That we never went anywhere and that she should have left me ages ago.

For any person to be made to feel so inadequate sexually, visibly, personally to the point that I'd made her skin crawl has never left me. This was my partner who I would have trusted with my life. Now in just five minutes flat I realised I never knew her at all.

Luke made it clear that he would not have returned to our Crisis Centre if he had been allocated to a different member of our team after the first assessment. In those early days, he could not have faced another person knowing the circumstances that had led to his crisis. He described feeling a huge sense of shame, which was a barrier to disclosure, 'I hid from everyone. The shame was too much to bear. I was a broken, inadequate human being who had previously thought I was loved and respected.' Additionally, there was the issue of trust. His trust in people had been profoundly damaged, and this was an additional reason why he only felt able to work with and build trust with one team member initially.

In order to help men such as Luke, who are the least likely to disclose their risk to anyone, we have had to go above and beyond what we would usually provide. It has always been our aim to reach people who would not usually seek help from any other source and whose silence about their suicidal feelings puts them at greater risk.

We are sometimes asked how this is achievable, how only one member of staff can support someone who is in crisis. It has been feasible because the period of intense crisis usually only lasts a short time. This is the period where they may require daily support. The need for daily support has never lasted more than ten days. The amount of contact reduces quite naturally after this. Not all of the male clients who only felt able to be supported by one staff member wished to come in every day. It is true that there have been times when I have come into work on my day off for an hour to support someone. This has been my choice and it is not something I have ever asked a member of our team to do. It is very important that all members of our team have adequate rest and time away from work. We would also never expect that other organisations should feel under any obligation to go above and beyond what they usually provide. However, if we are looking at why all clients under our care have survived, then such measures may have been a contributory factor.

The ability to only disclose information about their crisis to one person also meant that they ruled out using telephone helplines, as this would involve speaking to a different person each time they phoned.

After the acute phase of Luke's crisis had subsided, it was possible to involve a second team member in his care, and he was also able to connect and build trust with her.

WARMTH, CARE AND CONNECTION

Our male clients are far less likely than our female clients to disclose their suicidal thoughts to family members or friends. We actively encourage them to do so, but many still feel unable to. Some of our male clients say that they are used to supporting everyone else in their family. They are the person to whom everyone else turns in a crisis. They may feel a pressure to always remain in this role – that of the protector, the person who looks after everyone else. Many feel that they would be 'burdening' family members if they told them. Some men in their middle years and older men explain to us that all their surviving family members are younger than them. They have no family members in their age group or older, and they do not wish to disclose their crisis to their children or nephews and nieces. Many men also feel unable to tell their friends because they grew up in a time when showing emotion was less accepted.

As a result, many of our male clients do not receive care and support from family members during their crisis. The absence of family involvement makes it even more important that crisis services which support men provide warmth, connection, empathy, acceptance and a caring approach. This is, of course, in the context of a professional relationship which has clear boundaries.

NOT AN ANONYMOUS SERVICE

One of the primary reasons that men come to us in crisis is because of a relationship breakup or the death of a partner. At a time when they may feel bereft and alone, the connection they build with us and the warmth and care they receive become very important. Although the confidentiality of our service is important to them, they say they are not seeking an anonymous service. They want to be known to and feel connected with the team members.

John accessed our services after the breakup of his marriage. He explained, 'When I came to the Suicide Crisis Centre I found understanding and human warmth. I found empathy. The reassurance of another person caring that I continued to exist and survive. That was massive to someone feeling so isolated.'

After a relationship breakup, our female clients are much more likely to take comfort from the support of their friends than our male clients are. It is not just that men find it harder to open up to their friends and colleagues about how they are feeling, they also describe how the reaction of their friends and colleagues sometimes actively prevents them from doing that.

John explained:

Friends, family and work colleagues backed off. They could see my vulnerability, and it felt like they were judging me as a person. I wasn't the strong reliable person they thought I was. I felt they could see all my inadequacies. I felt broken and alone.

There may be many reasons why they withdrew – fear, not feeling comfortable at the prospect of talking about emotional issues or personal matters, or not knowing how to help or support. However, there is sometimes a sense of shock that the person is presenting in a way that they have never witnessed previously. This does not only apply to men who experience suicidal crisis. One of our female clients experienced a similar response from a male friend. He spoke of his shock that she was in suicidal crisis. He spoke in terms of having lost the 'strong person' he had known up to that point. Significantly, though, she was able to challenge in her own mind the validity of what he was saying. She did not feel that a suicidal crisis was a reflection of a lack of strength. Our male clients have found it harder to do this. If their male friends suggest that they are 'not the strong person' they knew previously, they are much more likely to absorb this and feel that their suicidal crisis makes them 'less of a man'.

The phrase 'stay strong' is used widely, particularly as an expression of encouragement, when someone is going through difficult times. Increasingly, we see it on suicide prevention websites and on social media. If someone is known to be in suicidal crisis, friends frequently email or text the phrase 'stay strong'. My concern is that the emphasis on 'strength' risks putting pressure on the person to feel that they should rely on themselves rather than to feel that they can seek help and support. I would wish to encourage men in crisis to feel able to be vulnerable and seek support.

— CHAPTER 8 —

THE TEAM

TEAM MEMBERS: PERSONAL QUALITIES, SKILLS AND TRAINING

Finding the right team members to work with our clients was vital. We needed to find people who were not just highly skilled and confident to work with clients who may be at high risk of suicide. They also needed to have the personal qualities that we were looking for. We were seeking individuals who were kind, caring, empathic, understanding, sensitive, respectful towards our clients and non-judgemental.

Although it was important that they had a counselling background, there is usually a greater 'distance' between a counsellor and client than there is between our team members and clients. It was important that counsellors coming to work for us had an ability to adapt to our way of working and that they felt comfortable with a professional relationship which included caring openly for clients.

All but one of our team members who work with clients are fully qualified counsellors accredited by the British Association for Counselling and Psychotherapy. This is the most widely known accrediting body for counsellors in the UK. They have additional training in suicide intervention skills (a course recommended by the Department of Health). This course demonstrates what questions to ask to determine someone's risk of suicide and what to do to ensure that they are kept safe. Our advising psychiatrist was able to assist with aspects of our training and arranged for us to have additional input on assessing suicide risk from a clinical lead within an NHS mental health service. Indeed, all our advising clinicians have contributed to our knowledge about risk assessing and risk management. This combination of counselling training and input from mental health clinicians ensures that we are skilled and confident to work with clients who may be at high risk of suicide.

Our team members have differing specialist skills which they bring to their role. Some have previously worked extensively in bereavement counselling. Hilary, in particular, has a huge amount of experience in this area. Others have specialised in working with younger people or in addiction services. Some of our team have additional work experience which is extremely helpful to clients and to our organisation. Geoff, for example, is a qualified counsellor who has also volunteered for many years for Citizens Advice, a charity that provides advice to the public on a wide range of issues, including legal matters and welfare benefits.

They were drawn to work for our charity for different reasons. Janie explained what led her to become involved:

> I read a job advertisement for the role of team member which explained about the ethos of the charity as well as the specific role. I was intrigued by Joy's approach and her commitment to the client, and flexibility to adapt to their needs so that no one 'slips through the net' as they can do so often in other services. Despite my many other commitments at the time, this still felt like something I was compelled to do. Working with suicide risk had been discussed during my counselling training, and I knew it would be something I would need to face with courage. I feel strongly that when a person is in a dark and lonely place, they need support from someone who is not frightened by this, but able to listen without adding their own anxiety to the client's.

She spoke about her contribution to our charity:

> My role within Suicide Crisis has been primarily one of support
> and encouragement. I provide a safe space for the client to
> explore feelings they have been fighting to contain. I work
> proactively with them to find reasons to survive. They know
> that I care about them and that I value them during the times
> when they are unable to see their own worth.

Janie feels that her way of working draws much from the
person-centred approach within counselling, and it includes
'encouraging self-compassion and fostering self-tolerance'.
This encourages the person not to be self-critical but to try to
treat themselves with the same kindness and care they might
show to another person.

Some of our clients feel that clinicians have not always taken
this approach within mental health services. Their recollection
is of staff tending to point out what they were not doing, which
at times led them to feel that they were 'failing'.

One of our clients worked full time, but at weekends her
children sometimes went to stay with their grandmother. Our
client always felt much more at risk of suicide at these times.
She would often spend the Saturday in bed, doing very little.
Her mental health team felt that it would be more helpful for
her to be out of bed doing things, being active and productive.
They make a valid point and this is of course in keeping with
the distraction techniques which can be so effective – keeping
mind and body occupied. However, if, after encouragement to
do so, the person is finding that they can't, then it is important
that they don't hear repeated messages of how they should be
doing something different. In such circumstances, it can be
helpful to recognise that the person is doing the best that they
can. Furthermore, in this case, the young woman demonstrated
that she was able to maintain her safety in bed on these days
and indeed her survival was our priority at that point. As she

had spoken of ending her life at a particular outdoor location which was known as a 'suicide hotspot', I took some reassurance from the fact that she was safe at home in bed.

Additionally, she was a mother of young children and worked full time. Life was demanding and at times exhausting, and indeed she frequently described being exhausted. Resting in bed all day could be restorative. My view was that her safety and survival were paramount, and if staying in bed all day was keeping her safe at times, then that was a positive outcome. Furthermore, staying in bed could be seen as a form of self-care: she was giving both body and mind time to rest.

Hilary gave her view about her role within our charity:

> Overall, the person-centred approach is most definitely the basis for the team member/client relationship within Suicide Crisis. However, at the same time we need to be very direct in order to recognise whether they are having suicidal thoughts and if those thoughts have become more active – and if so, what they are and how, why and when the thoughts arose. The professional relationship becomes more solution-focused which would never normally be part of a person-centred relationship. However, the much more direct approach must be done with a great deal of compassion, caring and understanding. Because we are so compassionate with clients, they are very much aware of how much Suicide Crisis cares about them.

Geoff added:

> We support clients on an open-ended basis to help them feel able to face the future again, value themselves and recover from their crisis.
>
> It is very rewarding when people I have supported feel able to move forward with their lives, override feelings of desperation and start to value themselves. In many instances, they have not made progress with other interventions or mental health services.

As well as having different skills and backgrounds, our team members also bring their own individual, personal qualities to the role. Previously I have mentioned gentleness and how highly I value this quality in a person. However, this sometimes leads to people making an assumption that all our team members are gentle in nature. Many of them are, but not all. Every member of our team is different.

A client may connect better with some members of our team than others. As we know our staff well, we are usually able to predict which team members might work well with a client when we are assessing them initially. The team has changed very little since the early days, and so in most cases we have been working together for several years now. This has led to a strong, cohesive group of individuals. We trust and support each other, and value each other's different skills, abilities and personal qualities. We also like each other and enjoy spending time in each other's company.

The majority of our team members who work with clients are female. We did not set out to have a predominantly female team, but a number of our male clients have told us that they feel more comfortable receiving support from a female. It is particularly men in their middle years or older who have stated this preference. They have explained subsequently that they would have found it more difficult to disclose information about the reasons for their suicidal crisis to a man – or to be vulnerable in front of another man. Luke explained:

> If I had seen a male counsellor that first day, would I still be here? I'm not sure if I would or could have opened up to a bloke. For a guy to admit vulnerability, to portray anguish and sorrow, to weep openly, lay undone with no control to hide feelings or emotions...I'm not sure if I could have done that in front of a man.

SUPPORT STAFF AND THEIR VITAL ROLE IN HELPING TO SAVE LIVES

A team of volunteer drivers works alongside us, providing invaluable support. We have built a strong bond of loyalty and trust between us, which is extremely important. A team member and a driver often go out to situations that may be unpredictable and where the client may be at high risk of suicide. The driver's focus is on the safety and well-being of the clients who we are going to see, but also on our safety and well-being.

There are times when it is hugely advantageous for a team member to be driven to the home of a client, rather than have to drive themselves, particularly in situations where a client is at imminent risk. It means that they can talk on the phone to the client while they are travelling to their home, to ensure that the client remains safe until they reach them.

Some of our volunteer drivers have taken a basic counselling course and undertaken suicide intervention skills training. This allows them to assist the team member in some situations. On a regular visit to a known client, the driver will usually wait in the car. However, if the team member arrives at the client's home and finds an unexpected situation, they may seek the assistance of the volunteer driver. They may arrive at a person's home and find that it is important to involve other organisations immediately. At this point, the team member can make phone calls to appropriate agencies while the volunteer driver talks to and provides reassurance to the client.

On one occasion, I collected the keys to the client's home from the key safe at the side of her property and let myself in as usual. I found her lying on the bed with blood on her face. She was able to explain that she had sustained a fall, but she had apparently managed to make her way to her bed afterwards. She had consumed a large amount of alcohol, which had led to her falling. She was only able to speak a few words at a time and was clearly confused, so on this occasion Allan, the volunteer driver, phoned emergency services to ensure their prompt arrival, while I remained talking to our client. It was important on this occasion that a person she knew and trusted remained by her side.

Our drivers are highly dedicated to the work that they are doing. I recall that one night a young woman had made contact with us for the first time and we felt that we needed to go out to see her immediately, because we were concerned about her risk of suicide that night. I contacted the different volunteer drivers but, unusually, none was available. One of them was able to take me out to the young woman's home, but could not stay. I felt as confident as I could be that I would be safe to be left alone with her, but my usual 'partner' who accompanied me to see clients in their homes was concerned when he heard about this. 'I can't believe I am on a night out in Bristol with this situation going on. I'm coming back,' he said.

It was 5am before we felt it safe to leave the young woman. My 'partner' and I left her home and contemplated each going to our respective homes to catch up on a few hours' sleep before the next working day began. However, we found ourselves sitting in his car, talking, instead. I think that much of the bond between team members and drivers has been formed in that time following an incident or after going to see a client at imminent risk.

We are extremely indebted to our volunteer drivers who provide such vital support to us and work so tirelessly to ensure our safety as well as that of our clients.

CHANGING THE POWER BALANCE BETWEEN CLINICIAN AND SERVICE USER

All our team members receive supervision from practitioners who have many years' experience of providing it either in a clinical or counselling setting. The regular supervision sessions provide support for the team member, as well as an opportunity to reflect on their work and to learn and develop in the role. There are also 'debriefing' sessions: the opportunity to talk to a senior member of staff after each 'shift' about what has happened and the impact on the team member. If necessary, our supervisors can also be available at short notice if there has been a particularly challenging session or incident. For example, a client may have disclosed something particularly distressing in the course of a session, or an emergency call-out may have been particularly harrowing. Our clinical advisers may become involved, too. Our advising psychiatrist and other clinicians have on occasions provided additional support to the team member, even though this was not anticipated as part of their role initially.

An advising psychiatrist has been involved in our charity since the early days. A retired psychiatrist advised us during the setting-up stage, in the months before we opened. Then Gideon, our current advising psychiatrist, took over the role. He has a wealth of experience, including working in prisons, and is now the lead psychiatrist in a drugs and alcohol service. Prior to that, he worked in an NHS community team for patients with more severe and enduring mental health diagnoses. One of the first things he said to me on joining our organisation was: 'Use me as an encyclopaedia', and we certainly do, whether it is in relation to learning more about psychiatric diagnoses, or questions about mental capacity or other mental health legislation. Our advising clinicians make themselves available to answer questions at very short notice, for which we are profoundly grateful. Gideon explains his role as follows: 'My role really is that of "walking textbook", providing opinions on specific subjects, especially on scientific and medico-legal matters, which I feel I am most experienced in. It is important that the advice I give is useable, precise and robust.'

Our clinicians do not work directly with our clients and never know their identity when we go to them for specific advice. It probably helps that they all work for NHS Trusts outside our immediate locality, thus avoiding a situation where they might recognise a patient from our description of a particular presentation or situation.

An interesting aspect of our organisation is how the power balance can be viewed as a reversal of that which exists within mental health services. A 'psychiatric patient' created and runs our organisation, choosing to employ psychiatrists and other clinicians to contribute to our work and give advice about particular issues. In the early days, Gideon would frequently remind me that I am his boss.

Although this reversal of the power balance may seem quite radical for those of us who have experienced mental health services, Gideon explained to me that his specialist interest in addiction means that he is familiar with being managed by former service users. I went to visit him at the addiction service where he works, and he pointed out:

> Look at the colleagues I work with, many of whom have a 20-year history of drugs and alcohol addiction. Some of them have become my managers and give orders to me. I find it a privilege to receive instructions from those who were erstwhile patients. It is important to recognise how people who were in treatment can influence your practice.

In terms of our organisation, I perceive it as a levelling of power between former patient and advising clinicians. There is an equality between us, where we all have huge respect for each other's different strengths and abilities. We all learn from each other. The differing viewpoints make it an exciting and intellectually stimulating environment in which to work.

The members of our board of directors/trustees have a range of different skills and backgrounds. They have included a former governor of an NHS mental health service, managers of NHS services, clinicians, a hospital chaplain, counselling supervisors, an accountant and, very importantly, former clients who have used our services.

A former client who is a director/trustee commented:

Having been helped to survive by the charity, I feel very protective towards it. I was in crisis and held until recovery – watched over, trusted, supported and cared for. To understand fully why Suicide Crisis works, maybe you have to have lived the experience and come out the other end. To feel broken, put back together, then trusted to become part of that process (by becoming a trustee of the charity) gave me back some pride. It also gave me back some purpose, value and worth. The biggest difference between me and the other trustees is that I always think from the client's perspective, understanding the fragility of life with the experience of knowing what it's going to take to survive.

As well as all those who work regularly for our charity with such dedication, we receive excellent additional support from a number of professionals who provide short-term but invaluable input. Lawyers, in particular, have been willing to provide their services free of charge. They assisted us initially in drawing up the governing document for our charity and have on many occasions provided expert advice in areas of law, which has helped individual clients. Our treasurer, who is a very experienced charity accountant, initially heard about our charity when we approached him to ask if he would prepare our annual accounts. He took time to find out more about our charity, and this led to his offering to do the work free of charge. Later he became a trustee and our treasurer.

Once an organisation starts to demonstrate that it is making a difference, word spreads. Professionals hear about clients who have been supported. They may know someone who has been helped. This in turn creates a feeling of goodwill in the community towards the charity, and people want to contribute and help the work to continue. When we approached the owners of the town centre venue which we took over in the summer of 2014, we had no idea that they knew someone we had helped in the past. This led to them greatly reducing the rent for us. We didn't ask them to do this. They offered. Our original premises were expensive and so this decrease in rent made a significant difference.

The support of a local community can play a particularly important role in sustaining a charitable organisation in its early stages. We are extremely grateful for the kindness and assistance which have been shown to us by local professionals and organisations.

CHAPTER 9

WORKING WITH OTHER SERVICES

THE BARRIERS

When I stated my intention to set up a Suicide Crisis Centre, I encountered widespread scepticism. I was a person with mental health challenges who had recently experienced suicidal crisis myself. Many people were astonished that I was considering setting up a service to help other people in crisis. The attitudes I encountered served as a powerful reminder that preconceptions about people who have experienced mental illness are slow to change. Doubts about our ability to be competent professionals remain.

It still seems difficult for some people to understand that a person may have diminished capability when unwell, but that they can be immensely capable when well. Although my psychiatric diagnosis may be enduring, my episodes of mental ill health are not. My diagnosis of bipolar disorder means that I have depressive episodes at times, and these can be immensely challenging. At such times, I need to take time off work. When I am well again, I return to work and am able to work extremely productively.

It was particularly surprising to me that I encountered resistance to my plans from individuals within mental health services, the police and the clinical commissioning group (CCG), which funds local health services. Managers and senior managers within these organisations appeared highly sceptical. It was clear, however, that individual psychiatric clinicians welcomed the prospect of our service and were reaching out to us. The same applied to some police officers working in the front line, who reacted to us positively. When senior management within their organisations heard of such productive contact, it was discouraged, however.

A number of theories have been put forward to try to explain the attitude which mental health managers and some psychiatrists displayed in the early days towards our service, and in particular my role within it. At times, I felt they had extremely low expectations of what a person with mental health issues could achieve. Perhaps if you have only previously seen the person when they are having a mental health crisis, at a time when their capabilities may be limited, it becomes hard to imagine that they could be competent, capable and responsible when they are well.

Additionally, I have sometimes observed psychiatrists display what appears to be an underlying lack of optimism and hope in relation to patients. It is as if they do not expect that patients will act well in a given situation. When I accessed my psychiatric records, I found notes relating to a professionals' meeting in 2013 where a psychiatrist voiced concerns that my own experience of mental health services would lead me to express a negative view about the services to our clients, thus deterring them from using them. He even suggested that I might encourage them to complain about services and that I would somehow generate unrest among patients locally. There was no assumption that I would act professionally, nor that the well-being and safety of our clients would be my priority. As a competent professional, part of my role is to actively encourage our clients' use of mental health services. Additionally, the fact that the services did not work for me did not lead me to form generalised opinions about them. My conclusions were that some of us need a different type of service, not that mental health services were 'failing' us. Even when I was struggling to engage with them, I still recognised that many people thrive under their care.

This lack of belief that patients will act well, or in the interests of others, seemed to prevail when we were exploring the possibility of setting up a PTSD group within our Trauma Centre. We run a separate Trauma Centre, which provides early intervention to help prevent clients from going into crisis. The Centre offers predominantly individual support, but a number of clients suggested that a PTSD group would also be extremely beneficial to them. It would provide additional support as well as an opportunity to meet others who had the same condition. However, the first psychiatrist we consulted about the group advised against it. She explained that there was a risk that the group members would talk about the detail of their traumas, which could of course be potentially retraumatising for them and for other members of the group. 'What if we created a ground rule for the group where participants are asked not to talk about the detail of their traumas?' I asked. 'They will anyway,' she said. 'You won't be able to stop them.'

We spent time working with another NHS clinician – the former clinical lead of a psychological therapies service – and she advised us on how to set up the group safely. The group members proved that the psychiatrist's assumptions were unfounded. We made it a rule that they should not talk about the detail of their traumas, explaining that it was to protect them and the other group members. Their response was to immediately endorse it. They did not want to do anything which risked harming or having a detrimental effect on the other group members. They were caring, responsible individuals who were concerned about the welfare and well-being of their peers. The fact that they had mental health issues should not lead professionals to presume that they would not be able to exercise self-control or be able to consider the impact of their actions on others. I sometimes wonder what those clinicians have witnessed over the years to make them lose faith in the ability of patients to act selflessly and in the interests of others, and to have so little expectation that patients will act responsibly or with good intent.

In terms of attitudes displayed by managers within the local mental health service, it has been suggested that they focused on promoting the idea that it was 'inadvisable' for a former psychiatric patient to take on the role of running a Crisis Centre because they were motivated by fear. Some individuals who held senior roles in other organisations suggested that the managers perceived our service as a threat. Perhaps this was because it appeared to risk challenging the usual order: the psychiatrist and the psychiatric service were the ones who were traditionally 'in charge', not patients. That may have seemed alarming, or at least unsettling.

Some wondered whether they may have interpreted the setting up of our Crisis Centre as a direct challenge on my part, because it was clear that it was my own experience of services and the wish to provide something different that had been a driving force. Perhaps they viewed it as an implicit criticism, a statement that what they had provided was 'not enough' or 'not effective'. However, it was always my intention that our Suicide Crisis Centre would provide an alternative service, not a replacement. It was intended to meet the needs of those who would never access mental health services, as well as provide something different for those who had not thrived under them.

There is a much greater understanding now on the part of clinicians that we are providing something which complements their services. This change has come about gradually, as they started to see that some of their patients were using both services, and that this combination of services was meeting their needs. Patients were continuing to use mental health services for their ongoing care in the community but were coming to us when in crisis. The clinicians could see that we were actively encouraging our clients to continue to engage with mental health services. It was clear to them that we respected their work and recognised their essential role. They were also hearing their patients speaking positively about their experiences under our care and this was providing strong evidence to challenge the preconceptions of their managers.

The response from senior police officers and, at times, more junior officers in those early days was perhaps even more negative. There were officers who openly questioned the advisability of a 'mental health patient' running a Suicide Crisis Centre.

I was particularly shocked by an encounter with the police in the first few months. One of our clients phoned us one evening to explain how his suicidal intent was being fuelled by his fear of a group of individuals who were targeting him. As well as having mental health issues, he had physical disabilities. The group would hammer on the walls of his flat and shout abuse through his letterbox. They had become friendly with one of the other residents in his block of flats, and this allowed them access to the building. They had issued multiple threats against him, which made him fear for his personal safety.

I phoned the local police force and asked them to attend his address to ensure his safety and to provide help. The incident was passed to a senior police officer. It was puzzling to me that his focus appeared to be on me rather than on the individual at risk. In raising this with the police afterwards, I received a letter informing me that incorrect information had been placed on their computer systems. They advised me that this incorrect operational information appeared on their screens whenever I made a phone call to them. My name and phone number would generate the following alert for the officer taking the call:

Caller Joy Hibbins. She claims she is part of the Suicide Crisis team and asks for various welfare checks. She isn't part of the team, and it appears that she is herself a MH patient.

This operational information appeared to indicate a deeply entrenched prejudice on the part of some senior officers towards people with mental health issues. It was apparently not possible for some of them to recognise that a person with a psychiatric diagnosis could also be a competent professional. The officer appeared to assume that I was experiencing delusions that I was part of the Suicide Crisis team.

This information was on police computers for several weeks before it was corrected.

There were, of course, some officers who were supportive from the early days. They wished to become actively involved and work with us, but my impression was that they were hampered by more cautious senior officers.

We saw police officers' attitudes change as they started to hear more and more positive feedback from people who had used our services. They were encountering our clients in various situations. I knew that perceptions were starting to alter when a client reported to us that she had told police officers that she was receiving support from Suicide Crisis, and one of them had replied: 'Oh, yes, we know Joy and her team. They help a lot of people.'

The leader of a well-established charity gave me a piece of advice shortly before we started providing services. She could see that I was battling against significant scepticism and doubt. Her recommendation was not to verbally challenge the cynics: 'You do not have to respond to the critics directly. Let your work speak for itself.' It was excellent advice. It made me realise that the best approach was to quietly get on with my work, and that I should avoid expending my energies in trying to convince sceptics of the merits of my plans. The results of our work have provided a much more eloquent and powerful response to the sceptics than I ever could.

In terms of accessing funding, my mental health issues appeared to create a barrier in the early days. We approached our local CCG, the organisation that funds health services and some charitable services in our region. They invited us to a meeting, and I was asked to provide a lot of information about my mental health and the treatment I was accessing. The questions felt intrusive, and it was a difficult experience. Their conclusion was that they would not fund us at this time, and they commented, 'Let's see if people use your services.'

The lack of CCG funding was an advantage to us in the end. It led us to generate our own funding from donations and small grants, and this allowed us to retain our independence. It also meant that our services could evolve in those first few weeks and develop into a model which really met the needs of our clients. We were answerable to them, not to local commissioners.

As the commissioners saw the progress and success of our organisation, their attitudes changed, and they expressed an interest in funding us. However, we were concerned that this might lead to a loss of independence and autonomy, and we decided not to pursue this stream of funding. We feel that it is probably advisable that the original model remains 'untouched' and unchanged by external bodies.

WORKING IN PARTNERSHIP

In terms of our professional contact with mental health services, we have an important role in helping and encouraging clients to access them. There are times when we may feel that their presentation requires the opinion and input of a psychiatric clinician. This does not only occur in an emergency situation, where there is an immediate risk to life. We may feel that their presentation suggests that ongoing psychiatric input would be beneficial.

Paul was experiencing what appeared to be severe dissociative episodes. At times, he would find himself in unfamiliar places and would have no idea how he had arrived there. On one occasion, he suddenly became aware of someone shouting at him. To his astonishment and bewilderment, he found that he was standing in a road, listening to a lorry driver angrily castigating him for having stepped out in front of his vehicle's path. On another occasion, he was alarmed to have woken up and found himself in bed holding a kitchen knife in each hand. He had no recollection of having left his bed to collect these knives.

We were extremely concerned about the risks posed by these episodes. We were, however, relieved that Paul had felt able to disclose them to us, particularly as he had not yet felt able to tell a medical professional. When he described the episodes to us, he did so in the context of expressing a fear that they indicated that he was losing his sanity. He was very fearful of this possibility. After we explained that there could be several reasons why he was experiencing these symptoms and that one possible explanation was dissociation, he told us that he felt a massive sense of relief. One of our roles can be to assist people in accessing mental health services who would not otherwise have done so, perhaps because they would have been afraid to, as Paul was.

We also encounter clients who have been trying to access mental health services themselves, but have encountered barriers. This happens quite frequently in the case of people who have mental health issues and are also using drugs or alcohol. The mental health service will sometimes say that they need to access addiction services instead, and our role is sometimes to advocate for the client to have psychiatric input as well.

We consider it immensely important to share information about clients with other services whenever possible. The trusting relationship which we build with clients encourages disclosure, and it is not unusual for them to share information with us that they have not revealed to other organisations. If a client is under mental health services and we think it would be helpful or important for them to know the information, we seek the client's consent to share it. In most cases, they will agree to this quite readily. Often the client has not deliberately chosen to withhold the information from mental health services. It has simply been difficult to say or they have needed to be in the right environment, in a place where they feel safe and have plenty of time to disclose the information.

Additionally, when such a small team is having daily contact with a client, as we are, it is possible to build a more in-depth knowledge and understanding of what is happening to them. We may observe things which have not been picked up by mental health services and this is important to share, with the client's consent.

My preference is usually to share this type of important but non-urgent information by email. This allows the clinician to read it at a time which is convenient to them. They can then easily forward the email to other involved mental health clinicians or upload the document directly to the patient's psychiatric record.

We also share information regularly with GPs, with the client's consent, and we know that they really welcome this. They may see the client fairly infrequently and when they do see them, they may have only a ten-minute appointment in which to gather information. We are spending many more hours with the client and this enables us to form a very detailed understanding of them and of the issues affecting them.

When a client is under a number of services, it may become clear to us that some of the agencies involved only have partial information. In these circumstances, and with the client's permission, we ensure that all the involved agencies have the information. This can be particularly important in the case of their psychiatric diagnosis. Our organisation and the mental health service may be aware of their diagnosis, but addiction services may be entirely unaware, and it is important that they have this information. In the past, addiction services were part of the NHS, which meant that their clinicians had potential access to information in a person's mental health records.

They were all part of the same service. Now, however, they are entirely separate organisations and, in our experience, this can lead to gaps in information.

In some cases, even the local mental health service may not have knowledge of the person's diagnosis, perhaps because they have moved from a different area. In Ben's case, he had been diagnosed with a personality disorder when he was in prison. The only reason we knew this was because his mum disclosed it to us. She was very concerned that he was not receiving any mental health care in the community and that his situation was deteriorating rapidly. She had seen a letter from psychiatric services at the prison which gave information about his diagnosis. The local mental health teams were of the opinion that he had no need of their services and that addiction services were the most appropriate source of help for him. The letter provided clear evidence to the contrary, and we were able to ensure that this was shared, with Ben's consent.

Similarly, if the client is in supported housing, the staff are not always aware of all relevant information, including diagnosis. This became apparent to us from our research into deaths by suicide. Lack of information sharing between organisations is a recurrent theme at inquests. It was apparent in Shane's case. He had just moved to high-support housing, because he was vulnerable and had complex needs. At his inquest, it was revealed that staff working at the high-support housing complex were entirely unaware of his psychiatric diagnosis. They documented in their records that he had no mental health issues. Other organisations had been aware of his mental health needs, but had apparently not shared the information. Similarly, information about his risks had not been shared between the different organisations involved in his care. Staff at his new accommodation were unaware of his recent suicide attempts.

The coroner issued a Prevention of Future Deaths (PFD) report after Shane's inquest. There is a statutory duty to make reports to an organisation where the coroner believes that action should be taken to prevent future deaths. The PFD issue which the coroner identified after Shane's inquest related to the sharing of information: when multiple agencies are involved in a person's care, which organisation takes the lead in information sharing?

This was an extremely important PFD report and we welcomed it. There have been several occasions where we have needed to take the lead in ensuring that information has been shared between different agencies. My impression is that statutory services' understandable wish to protect clients' confidentiality has sometimes prevented them from realising that many clients are extremely willing for the different organisations involved in their care to share relevant information. You just need to ask them. They will usually readily consent, in our experience. Clients tend to perceive this sharing of information as being likely to improve the care they receive and ensure that they are better protected, because relevant information about their risks is being shared, too.

Our joint working with the police happens most usually in emergency situations when a person is at immediate risk. If we receive a phone call from a person who is at a location where they could end their life within seconds, particularly if it is their first contact with us, we will alert the police via a 999 call, because they are likely to reach them faster than we can. We remain on the phone to the person, with the police on another line. The police tend to prefer that we continue to talk to the person, while they work to locate them. This is our preference, too. A senior police officer in their control room will direct officers to allow one of our team to continue to be the sole communicator with the person at risk. On one occasion, I heard a senior officer in the control room say to his colleagues: 'Just let them do their stuff', a phrase which my colleagues rather liked. 'Doing our stuff' involves working to keep the person connected with us. We are focusing on rapidly building rapport with them and trying to find what has led to their current crisis. We are 'holding' them while the police make their way to them. We are also trying to glean relevant information which can help to locate them because their precise location may not be immediately apparent. All the while, we are keeping the police aware of every development and any important information which could help them. At the same time, the police are passing information to us and will sometimes make a direct request for us to try to find out a specific piece of information from the person.

Sometimes both the police and Suicide Crisis may attend the same incident, when there is an immediate risk to life. This is more likely to happen when the person is a known client and they are in their own home. If we are making a home visit, and the client fails to answer their door, we may have concerns that they may have already made a suicide attempt and we request the intervention of the police. The police can force access to the home.

If a known client contacts us stating an imminent intention to end their life in their own home, we may request police attendance because often they can reach the client minutes before we can. If we have enough available staff, we can then attend the client's home and support them, and at this stage the police may leave, unless we have concerns about the person's mental capacity and feel that they need a mental health assessment. In those circumstances, the police also have a responsibility to ensure the person's safety and that they are assessed by a mental health professional.

In terms of working with other charities, sharing specialist knowledge is beneficial to all of us. Local charities frequently approach us to request that we provide input into the training of their staff, to enable them to feel more confident in knowing how to respond when a client discloses that they are having suicidal thoughts. Similarly, it is important that our team gains as much knowledge as we can about specialist areas such as domestic violence or addiction from the relevant charities in our region.

Sometimes an employee of a local charity will phone us to ask for immediate advice about a client who is with them at the time. They are concerned about the individual's suicide risk and are not sure what action to take. We speak to both the employee and their client to assess the current situation and their risk and then advise on the best course of action.

Working closely with other organisations is extremely important to ensure the best outcomes for clients. However, there are times when we may need to stand alone. Occasionally, we may need to take a different stance from those agencies with which we work, because we believe that it is in the best interests of the client.

We had been supporting Jenna for several weeks. Her situation was complex and it was important that she left her current council accommodation. All the other agencies involved in her care were of the opinion that she should give up her dog, because he was proving to be a barrier to her accessing alternative accommodation. The council had very few properties for single people which allowed dogs. However, we knew that Jenna's dog was an important protective factor against her suicide. She was devoted to him and described him as being like her own child. A member of our team, who was supporting her, expressed her concern that Jenna's risk of suicide would increase markedly if she was forced to give him up. When I voiced our concerns to the other agencies, one of them replied, 'It is important that we are all on the same page, giving the same message to the client.' I remember thinking quietly, 'Not in this case.' We immediately started taking action ourselves by speaking directly to social housing providers, which provide low-cost housing for people with specific needs. To our immense relief, one of those organisations was able to offer her accommodation which permitted her to keep her dog.

Working with mental health clinicians and services in other parts of the UK has become important to us. They contact us quite frequently, either to gain learning about how we work or to ask us to contribute to their staff training. They sometimes invite us to contribute to the continuing professional development of psychiatrists and other clinicians. On other occasions, they wish to gain learning to inform new crisis services which they plan to set up. They, along with mental health commissioners and public health managers, frequently refer to our Suicide Crisis Centre as an example of 'best practice' and indeed the phrase was used in a letter which we received from the government last year. An extraordinary change of attitude towards our work has occurred in a relatively short timeframe. The acknowledgment and interest is such a marked contrast to the scepticism, doubt and resistance I encountered initially.

We also contribute to national partnerships. The government's adviser on suicide invited us to give a presentation about our work to the National Suicide Prevention Strategy Advisory Group, which he chairs. He subsequently asked us to attend a meeting with the Chair of the Parliamentary Health Select Committee, in relation to the government's suicide prevention strategy. We have also contributed to several meetings of the All Party Parliamentary Group on Suicide and Self-Harm. In this parliamentary group, Members of Parliament from all political parties work together in the interests of suicide prevention.

CHAPTER 10

THE FUTURE

ZERO SUICIDE: A HELPFUL TERM OR A HINDRANCE?

Our priority for the future is that all clients under our care continue to survive, as they have done for the past five years. Zero suicide is being talked about as an ambition by many people working in the field of suicide prevention. However, we tend not to use the phrase within our charity, other than retrospectively. We never set ourselves a goal of achieving zero suicide. My approach was simply that we would do everything we could for each individual to help them to survive. That has been our strategy since the first day. It is what we do every day.

One of my concerns about the current drive for zero suicide is the pressure which it may place on individual professionals. We already know that some psychiatrists and other clinicians may feel a disproportionate amount of individual responsibility after the death by suicide of a patient. This can become deeply damaging to their mental health. My concern would be that the focus within organisations on zero suicide may increase the risk of psychiatrists responding to a death in this way.

One of the reasons why we avoid using the phrase within our charity, when we are focusing on the future, is because I feel that it would place our team under too much pressure. We marked our fifth anniversary of providing services recently and I have been asked, 'Do you feel a huge pressure now to maintain this "record" of zero suicide?' I do not feel under pressure, because I know that we will simply do today (and tomorrow) what we have always done: our focus will be on doing all we can to ensure the survival of each individual.

Despite having some reservations, I can see the advantages to having 'zero suicide' as an ambition. It is my belief that all our clients can survive, and a zero-suicide ambition has at its heart a belief that each individual can survive suicidal crisis. Not all psychiatrists and clinicians appear to display such hope and optimism for their patients' survival, however. I still hear individual psychiatrists and doctors talking in terms of suicide being 'inevitable' for some of their patients. Promoting zero suicide as a concept serves to challenge and counteract this pessimism about individual patients' ability to survive.

During our research into deaths by suicide (Suicide Crisis 2018), we focused in particular on one young woman. Recently, I encountered one of the doctors who had treated her, and he told me that he had felt it was only a matter of time before she ended her life. I was astonished and deeply saddened to hear this. He seemed to suggest that nothing could have prevented the 'inevitable outcome' of her death by suicide. Our research identified several instances where there appeared to have been missed opportunities to help the young woman, or where things could have been done differently. We identified 14 learning points for the services involved in her care. I certainly did not feel that all possibilities and treatments had been explored.

He is not the only doctor who has spoken in such terms. A mental health professional said recently of one of our clients: 'He's the sort of person who'll be dead by the time he's 30.'

When a patient appears not to be improving or making progress under a service, there is a risk that clinicians may perceive them to be someone 'who cannot be helped'. In my opinion, the likelihood is that the person has simply not found the right kind of help yet. I would assume that a change of approach or even a change of service may be indicated. I do not believe we should ever reach the stage where we say, 'We have tried everything – there is nothing more to offer.'

The statutory mental health services may not work for everyone. We should not assume that this is a 'failing' on the part of the patient – the failure to engage or to be able to make good use of the service offered to them. We are all unique individuals, with different needs. The same service is unlikely to be helpful for everyone. I have heard patients being described as 'difficult to engage'. The perception is that the issue lies with the individual. I hope that this will change so that service providers start to say instead, 'We haven't been able to engage them.' This places some responsibility on the service, instead of attributing the full responsibility for engagement to the patient.

My experience of becoming a service provider has shown me the responsibility we bear in trying to provide a service which is tailored to the individual and which meets their needs. The onus is on us to try to help a person to engage – not simply to expect that they will. If someone is not engaging, I feel that it is the responsibility of the service provider to ask the questions: Why have we been unable to engage them? What do we need to do to make it possible for them to engage with our service? How do we ensure that we provide what they need, or if we feel we can't, then how do we help them to access a service which can?

Service providers bear a similar responsibility if a person is engaging but appears not to be improving or making progress. It is particularly when someone is self-harming or attempting suicide frequently that clinicians start to talk in terms of the inevitability of death.

When psychiatrists feel they can do no more for a patient, and start to view their death as inevitable, I believe they should be under an obligation to explore all other avenues outside their own local NHS Trust. I would like to see them routinely referring the patient out of county for an independent assessment. A psychiatrist in another part of the country can offer a fresh perspective and may draw up a completely different treatment plan which the local team can follow. Ideally this should be a specialist psychiatrist or a specialist unit.

It may also be that the treatment itself needs to be provided in another part of the country. Joanna, one of our former clients, told me:

> I was a sectioned patient in my local acute psychiatric hospital. I had narrowly survived an attempt to take my own life and was still actively suicidal and engaging in highly risky self-harm several times a day. Staff and my family felt powerless to know how to help me and I was later told by a charge nurse that I wasn't expected to walk out of the hospital alive.

Staff at the hospital decided to refer Joanna to a personality disorders unit situated in another part of the country. Residents are supported by specialist psychiatric staff, and Joanna felt that this made a significant difference, 'They are used to the rapid cycling of our moods here; they don't overreact when we get horrendously angry, they understand that we can feel extreme emotions and have truly dark thoughts without panicking and rushing in to medicate or restrain us.' Joanna added, 'There is a huge emphasis placed on patients supporting each other as much as having nurses support us.'

While a resident there, Joanna received an additional psychiatric diagnosis, 'That took me by surprise but I feel it explains a lot about me which the single diagnosis left unanswered.' She also received a type of therapy there which had never been offered to her in her own area: psychoanalytical therapy.

Joanna's experience shows how a change of approach and ethos, a different or additional diagnosis and different forms of treatment can transform a person's prospects of surviving.

It may be that the right form of care for the patient does not lie within psychiatric services. Charitable organisations can provide a wholly different approach and different techniques.

One of my hopes for the future is that all psychiatric clinicians will follow our approach; that they will be tenacious and explore as many avenues as possible to help the person survive. That may involve recognising that they are not the right people to help the individual. All of us working in a support or clinical role need to be aware of this. If the clinician starts to consider a patient's death to be inevitable, then this is the time to place that individual's care in the hands of another professional.

We need to persistently retain the belief that our clients and patients can survive. It is important that we hold on to hope for them. If they have lost all hope, then we need to retain it for them.

A significant proportion of psychiatric professionals feel uncomfortable with the phrase 'zero suicide' because of the increased pressure it may create. Perhaps in those circumstances we could promote instead a culture of 'infinite hope'. At the heart of this culture of infinite hope is a belief in every patient's ability to survive.

When we started providing services, I was told that some people under our care would die and that I must be prepared for that. We need to move away from that assumption. If a service provider accepts or assumes that some people under their care will die, then there is much more of a risk that they may stop trying to help after reaching a certain point. As well as maintaining abundant hope for those under our care, we need to be tenacious in helping them to survive. We need to work persistently to provide or find the help that they need. We should never stop trying. Infinite hope, endless endeavour.

Sometimes clients say to us, 'You don't seem to have given up on me.' We never will. They had experienced clinicians who had.

Although the future for our charity does not include specifying a zero-suicide ambition for our team, we are immensely grateful that all clients under our care have survived in the first five years that we have been providing services. In that sense, we can refer to having achieved zero suicide.

NEW CRISIS SERVICES

We are frequently contacted by people who want to set up a Suicide Crisis Centre in their own area. Indeed, barely a week passes without someone writing to me for advice about how to do so. One of the trustees of our charity has commented that I make the setting up of a Suicide Crisis Centre sound very easy when I speak about our work at conferences or when I have written articles for newspapers. I think the reason why it may appear that way is that I never focus on the many months of hard graft that preceded the opening of the Crisis Centre. That part of our history tends not to be particularly interesting for most people in the audience and so I avoid including it, but of course there was a huge amount of detailed work which was necessary to ensure that the Crisis Centre would be safe and effective.

It was an extremely ambitious project and so my approach was to break it down into a series of smaller tasks and focus on each one in turn. For example, one of the many tasks was to find an appropriate and safe venue. We needed to locate a building which would be easily accessible by public transport from all parts of the region in which we were operating. The layout of the building was also important. We needed to be able to look into all the rooms which would be used when seeing clients. It was important that the doors to the rooms all had a glass panel. A central reception area surrounded by client rooms meant that we could monitor what was happening in different rooms through the glass panels, if necessary. There was also a considerable amount of time spent on ensuring that the building was as safe as possible for our clients. The venue which appealed to us had previously been used for an entirely different purpose and so the proprietors had not needed to consider all the ways in which a person might harm themselves there. We needed to work carefully to minimise all possible ways in which anyone accessing our Crisis Centre could harm themselves.

Individuals who contact us are often in a rush to set up a service. This is understandable – there is huge unmet need. However, they risk missing out on the detailed preparation which will ensure the longevity of the project. Individuals have approached us for advice on setting up a service, and within weeks they are providing a service, having rented a room somewhere. However, within six months that service has disappeared. Taking care over every part of the setting-up stage will pay dividends, whether it is in identifying the right location and then making it as safe as possible, or in ensuring that your staff are well trained and supported as much as possible in their role.

My advice to anyone wishing to set up a similar centre would be to focus on creating solid foundations to ensure that the project survives. The months of thorough preparation and attention to detail allow the creation of firm foundations. Focus heavily on minimising risks. Make risk assessing your default setting, not just in all your plans and preparations for the Crisis Centre, but also in every situation that arises once the centre is up and running. I often hear comments made these days about organisations being too risk averse. As a crisis service, it is okay to be risk averse. Being risk averse has kept all our clients safe so far.

I am constantly in 'risk assess' mode, to the extent that I cannot switch off from it. I find myself, for example, monitoring risks when I am at conferences which we have not organised, or at meetings held by other organisations. I am conscious of the safety of everyone there. If someone in the audience walks out in the middle of a talk, it's possible that they just need to use the bathroom, or make a phone call because they have received an important message. However, the conferences

I attend relate to mental health and suicide, and so my first thought is: Are they okay? Have they been affected by the talk? Could they be at risk? Usually they will return promptly, but sometimes they don't. At a large county conference, we were all seated around tables and this allowed us all to talk during the breaks and find out a little about each other. When one of the people seated at our table walked out during a talk and never returned, I asked the conference providers to get in contact with her. Fortunately, they had her details and were able to call her to check she was okay. She did not find this intrusive. She was surprised but pleased that her absence had been noticed and that there was concern for her. Such concerns are legitimate. It is possible for someone who is vulnerable to be highly affected by a talk on suicide. It can increase their risk. Their vulnerability may not be apparent during the event.

In every situation which arises at work, I automatically ask myself the questions: What might go wrong in this situation? How might a person be adversely affected and how can we minimise the risk of that happening? Who else might be affected? How do we minimise the risks to them, too?

Being cautious about risk does not preclude having the courage to do things which have not been done before. It need not stifle innovation. It simply means that you try to minimise the risks to everyone. It doesn't prevent you from setting up the PTSD group which advising clinicians initially say is too risky. It simply means that you go away and think of a way that you can set it up which makes it as safe as possible.

When people in other parts of the UK hear about our services, they often use the phrase: 'This should be rolled out nationally.' They would like to see a similar Suicide Crisis Centre set up in every region. However, the funding system in our country makes this difficult. Funding for services tends to be localised. In England, each region has one (or more) clinical commissioning group which provides funding for health services, including hospitals, mental health services and also some charitable projects. This makes it unlikely that a service such as ours could be rolled out nationally. However, localised funding can provide the right environment for new and innovative local projects to flourish.

As well as being approached by individuals, we are also approached by health professionals and commissioners of services in other parts of the UK who would like to see our service replicated in their area. Finance is often a barrier, though. Our service is more complex than most, with its combination of Crisis Centre, home visits and emergency phone lines. There are models of service that are less complex and less costly than ours, for example a centre which provides a drop-in service. That is often the preferred model for local commissioners.

Perhaps our service will always remain something unique, which came about because of a particular set of circumstances, in a particular area, when a specific group of individuals came together. We have already seen, however, that some aspects of our service and some parts of our model have been replicated in other areas, for example in London.

In the future, I believe that there will need to be a greater focus on reaching people who are not accessing services – the people who are not seeking help when they are in crisis. Commissioners looking to fund new services often talk in terms of providing 'alternatives to emergency departments'. They wish to divert people in crisis away from hospital emergency departments or away from mental health crisis teams, because they are struggling to meet demand. The focus is on providing alternative provision for those already accessing services. This is extremely important because the alternatives may better meet their needs. However, there needs to be a greater focus on reaching and providing for those who would never access an emergency department or who would never seek help from their doctor or mental health service. We need to ensure that the 'alternatives' to these services are of a type which will attract people who are reluctant to seek help. We know that our service has been able to attract people who are 'off the radar' of other services and who state clearly that they would not have accessed them. If our model of service is too expensive to replicate, then there is a need to consider what alternative services should be created. I hope that political leaders will look at the aspects of our service which encourage those who are least likely to seek help to contact us and engage with us.

I hope that more people with lived experience will be trusted to take the lead in the setting up of new services. Although the contribution of people with lived experience is valued far more than it was, they are still more likely to merely be consulted about new crisis services, rather than given a leading role in their creation. It is far more likely to be commissioners or health service managers who take the lead. If our Suicide Crisis Centre had been designed by a commissioner or health service manager, it is highly unlikely that they would have developed the model that we have now, unless they also had lived experience of suicidal crisis.

We still seem to assume that it is psychiatrists and professors who hold the solutions to reducing the numbers of people who die by suicide. They are the ones to whom we instinctively turn. However, it is just as likely that people with lived experience will demonstrate the creativity and originality of thought that will lead to innovation in future crisis services.

Within our own organisation, we will continue to focus on doing everything we can for each individual to ensure that they survive, knowing that the world is a much better place for having them in it. As clients recover, they share with us their hopes and plans for the future. The most frequently stated future ambition is that they want to help other people: 'I just want to help as many people as I can.' Having experienced such acute emotional pain and suffering themselves, their greatest wish is to alleviate other people's suffering. They are the helpers, counsellors, teachers, lawyers and doctors of the future. Those of us who have been privileged to see the exceptional qualities which they possess know that they will enrich the lives of the people they encounter. All of us who work with people in suicidal crisis can take comfort that we leave the future in their capable hands.

For further information about the charity Suicide Crisis: www.suicidecrisis.co.uk.

REFERENCES

Appleby, L., Kapur, N., Shaw, J., Hunt, I.M. *et al.* (2016) *The National Confidential Inquiry into Suicide and Homicide by People with Mental Illness. Making Mental Health Care Safer: Annual Report and 20-year Review.* University of Manchester. Accessed on 24/07/2018 at www.research.manchester.ac.uk/portal/files/70178282/2016_report.pdf

Council of Europe. European Convention on Human Rights (amended 2010). Accessed on 25/07/2018 at www.echr.coe.int/Documents/Convention_ENG.pdf

Department of Health (1983) Mental Health Act. London: HMSO. Accessed on 20/06/2018 at www.legislation.gov.uk/ukpga/1983/20/contents

Department of Health (2005) Mental Capacity Act. London: HMSO. Accessed on 19/06/2018 at www.legislation.gov.uk/ukpga/2005/9/pdfs/ukpga_20050009_en.pdf

Health Select Committee (2016) *Oral Evidence: Suicide Prevention,* 8 November 2016, HC 300. London: House of Commons. Accessed on 19/06/2018 at http://data.parliament.uk/writtenevidence/committeeevidence.svc/evidencedocument/health-and-social-care-committee/suicide-prevention/oral/42994.html

National Institute for Health and Care Excellence (2009) Borderline Personality Disorder: Recognition and management. Clinical guideline (CG 78). Glossary: Dialectical Behaviour Therapy. Accessed on 19/06/2018 at www.nice.org.uk/guidance/cg78/ifp/chapter/glossary#dialectical-behaviour-therapy-sometimes-called-dbt

Suicide Crisis (2018) *Research into Deaths by Suicide in Gloucestershire.* (restricted report: for further information contact@suicidecrisis.co.uk).